Early Poems

By the author
Here
Black Orchid
Between the Root and the Flower
The Visitation
The Tradition
Song of Fear
The Ruined Cottage
Ciudad interior
Phantoms in the Ark
Mahoning
A Houseboat on the Styx
Rest on the Flight into Egypt
The End of the Age
Conflicting Desire

Translation
Children of the Quadrilateral: Selected Poems of Benjamin Péret
Testament for Man: Selected Poems of Gilberto Meza

Translation of works by Ludwig Zeller
Ludwig Zeller in the Country of the Antipodes: Poems 1964-1979
The Marble Head and Other Poems
The Ghost's Tattoos
Body of Insomnia and Other Poems
Rio Loa: Station of Dreams

Non-Fiction
Canada Illustrated
America the Picturesque

Non-Fiction written in collaboration with Theresa Moritz
The Pocket Canada: A Complete Guide to the World's Second-Largest Country
Leacock: A Biography
The Oxford Literary Guide to Canada
The World's Most Dangerous Woman: A New Biography of Emma Goldman
Stephen Leacock: His Remarkable Life

Early Poems

A.F. Moritz

Copyright © 2002 by A.F. Moritz

All rights reserved. No part of this publication may be reproduced, stored in a retrieval system or transmitted, in any form or by any means, without the prior written permission of the publisher or, in case of photocopying or other reprographic copying, a license from CANCOPY (Canadian Copyright Licensing Agency), 1 Yonge Street, Suite 1900, Toronto, Ontario, Canada, M5E 1E5.

Edited by Paul Vermeersch
Copy edited by Adrienne Weiss
Designed by Mike O'Connor
Cover Art by Ludwig Zeller

National Library of Canada Cataloguing in Publication Data

Moritz, A. F.
    Early poems

ISBN 1-894663-18-7

I. Title.

PS8576.O724E27 2002   C811'.54   C2002-900741-0
PR9199.3.M645E27 2002

The publisher gratefully acknowledges the support of the Canada Council, the Ontario Arts Council and the Department of Canadian Heritage through the Book Publishing Industry Development Program.

Printed and bound in Canada

Insomniac Press
192 Spadina Avenue, Suite 403
Toronto, Ontario, Canada, M5T 2C2
www.insomniacpress.com

Early Poems is for T.

Thus everything seems to bring us back to something which does not satisfy me and which I believe can in no way be satisfying. It is an assurance, one which is unable to commute itself into an evidence, and which perhaps would finally have to be compared to a prohibition or deprivation, since it is essentially the assurance of an impossibility. Let us attempt, even though it is hardly feasible, to describe this impossibility.

—Gabriel Marcel

Car j'ai vécu de vous attendre,
Et mon coeur n'était que vos pas.

—Paul Valéry

[For my life was my waiting for you,
And my heart was only your footstep.]

Table of Contents

Forewords

    Don McKay
    Shipwreck and Clear Sight: A.F. Moritz's *Early Poems*   14

    John Hollander
    Enriching Shadow: A.F. Moritz's *Early Poems*   17

New Poems (1974)

    Thinking About Dreaming   23
    A Woman   23
    The Choice   24
    Addiction   25
    The Hollow Wards   26
    In Reality   26
    Sweet Outrage   27
    She Speaks   27
    Difference of Opinion   28
    Like Water   29
    In Winter   29
    The First Chapters of Genesis   30
    Cab   31
    Soft Body   31
    They're Tearing Down the Walls Again Upstairs   32
    Blind Girl   33
    A Graceful Permission   33
    He Would Have Coursed the Doe   34
    Always on the Verge   34
    The Extreme Situation   35
    Relief Is at Hand   36
    Fragment   37
    The Fruits of Contemplation   38
    A Prison Diary   39

Here (1975)

    I   Here   43
         Today   43
         Betrayed Light   44
         The Art of Poetry   44
         Soliloquy of a Dreamer Absent from His Dream   45
         A Disease of the Throat   45

	At the City Dump	46
	The Destinies of Water	46
	The Old Man	47
	The Dead	47
	In the Well-Clipped Meadow	48
II	As Formerly	48
	The Uses of the Past	49
	Words to the Giantess	50
	Life of Determination	51
	Diaspora	52
	The Failed Disaster	52
	Desert Lament	53
	The Great Captain	54
	Genital Obstruction	55
	Symphonic	55
	The Imprint	56
III	My Method	57
	The Balloonist	58
	As I Understood It	58
	At the Hotel Oceano	59
	The Excursion	60
	The Hypnagogic State	61
	Reunion	64
	La Belle Epoque	65
	What Became of the Shepherd	66
IV	Whose Invention Was This	67
	Cut Flower	68
	The Future of Two Illusions	69
	Song	69
	Motive of the Journey	70
	The Birds Stay Far Away	71
	Loved Ones	73
	Believe It or Not, You Love Me	74
	One Lays His Hand Across Fissures	75
V	Shade	75
	A Leaf	76
	Recuperation	77
	Woodgate	77
	Morning Fragments	78
	Food for Three Days	79
	Eyes Pared to the Gleam	79

Moon	80
Anniversary in a Private Room	81
Saying Here	82

Black Orchid (1981)

Ulysses en Route	85
From Mean Families	86
Poem	87
Gone South	87
The Naturalist	89
Black Orchid	90
Levels	91
Northern Spring	92
The Pauses	95
On the Song of the Men	96
The Ravine	97
Second Person	98
The Wasp	99
These Dwarves	99
The Quest of the Egg	100
Exclusivity	101
Because the Wind Went Over Us	102
Stabbing	103
The Last Thing	104
Analysis	105
The Problem	106
Fields in the Air	107
Mansions	108
Among White Buildings	109
Before the Eyes of Statues	110
Romance	110
Memories of a Small Town Childhood	111
The Blue Gardenia	112
Deaf as a Post	115
Triumph of Epicurus	116
Aesthetic Distance	116
Modern Love	118
On the Bluff	118
The Ground	120
Under Crossed Swords	124
Dark Pocket	125
In the Maligned Museums	125
The Underground	126
The Smoker	128

With Satisfaction	129
Stranded	130
Diana	130
Episode from North American Folklore	131
The Katoliko	132
Nativity	132
Catalogue of Bourgeois Objects	133
The Voices in the Air	134

Between the Root and the Flower (1982)

A Narrow Silent Throat	137
The Window	137
In You the Sun	138
Witness to Dusk	139
Bell	139
Loud Light and Quiet Light	140
September	141
Oak Branch	141
Dark Man	143
A Natural History of Words	144
Desperate and Silent	145
Aftermath	146
Light of Flesh	147
Blue Lips	148
When Your Voices Go	148
A Secret	149
Permanence of Evening	150
Traveling	151
The Owl	152
Reeds	153
On the Preserved Body of an Inca Child	154
Only Deeper	154
If the Man	155
Foundation	156
Winter Garden	158
Jamaica	159
At the Tomb of André Breton	160
Eagles	160
Poem for Gilberto Meza	161
The Peasant's Soil	163
The Death of Francisco Franco	164

The Visitation (1983)

I	Music and Exile	173
	What They Prayed For	173
	Signs and Certainties	173
	The Crow	174
	Plunder	175
	On the Dial	175
	Chicory	176
	Pianoforte	176
	Capriccio of Roman Ruins	177
	Thoughts in a Bank Elevator	178
	Never Did I Let You Be Deceived	178
	Another Don Juan	179
	Letter Written from the Country	180
	Music and Exile	181
	Fire	183
	Fire Song	183
	The Scented Path	184
	A Pliant Hand	184
	Persephone	185
	In the Garden of Gethsemane	186
	The Prisoner	187
	Views	188
II	Areas	189
	1 Badlands	189
	2 City Park	190
	3 Lake Beach	190
	4 Creek Bank	191
	5 Creek Bank in Early Fall	191
	6 Creek Bank in Late Fall	192
	7 Ravine	192
	8 Remnant of a Woods	193
	9 Field at the Edge of Town in Early Spring	193
	10 Cavern	194
	11 Ocean Beach	194
	12 Fog Hollows in Town	194
III	Prayer for Prophecy	195
	Prayer for Prophecy	195
	Poverty	195

	Thanksgiving	196
	Locked Cupboard	197
	Gypsies	197
	Who Remembers	198
	The Mantis	199
	The Bushman in New York	200
	Africa	201
	The Beginning	202
	The Wheelwright	203
	The Air Hammer	205
	Court	206
	Before a Film	206
	Film in an Unknown Tongue	207
	The Ennui of Exegesis	208
	The War	209
	Prothalamium: Venus and Mars	210
	The Villa of the Humanist Collector	211
	Keats in Rome	212
	The Golem	213
IV	You, Whoever You Are	216
V	The Visitation	227

Author's Note   237

Shipwreck and Clear Sight:
A.F. Moritz's *Early Poems*

Don McKay

When you heft a volume of such weight and significance as this one collecting A.F. Moritz's early poems, it is understandable if it *is* volume that first impresses you—the sheer size of the accumulated achievement, the *oeuvre* or corpus, over a baker's decade of writing, 1966–77. But my guess is that such official terms quantifying art will rapidly give way to a sense of teeming abundance, and you will be more likely to reach for expressions like yard sale, attic, rag-and-bone shop (nodding to Yeats), dump (nodding to Stevens), menagerie, or, to deploy the metaphor used by the poet and Ludwig Zeller for their poem-and-collage collaboration, ark. That would be my choice to characterize *Early Poems* as well; it suggests live cargo, animal energies en route, and an ingeniously constructed craft which sustains life—not a bad summation of the insides of the book.

Two things hit me at once when I read Al Moritz: a sense of shift, of incipient metamorphosis which is everywhere in the poems, and an awareness that they are grounded in a deep intellectual and moral commitment. Those may seem contradictory on the surface, and especially if that first thing gets confused with postmodern freeplay, as it has come to be known. Instead, it's the consequence of the poet's profound anarchism, which denies the usual structures of knowing in the interests of opening a wider, phenomenal, sense of the real. Reading these poems, we are always crossing between accepted realms of experience—in fact often situated in that condition of betweenness, on a ferry thinking about dreaming (as in the poem so titled) and dreaming about thinking. At each point, one senses, the phrase is free, ready to slip across another border, and generally not with a lot of hoo ha and flashing of documents; rather it's as though the customs officers had turned smoothly into smugglers offering access to many possible worlds.

That ease and calm are important. When a person thinks of other radical romantics—Shelley, say, or Rimbaud, or Hart Crane (like Moritz a native of Trumbull County, Ohio) it often seems that the poet's heroism is the real story, not the process of imaginative engagement, as is the case with the poetic ark in question. One way of putting it would be to say that, in these early poems we do not so much experience the birth of the exotic (certainly part of the buzz, for me, with all three of those distinguished forbears of Al's) as the death of the banal. The aim of the imaginative crossing seems to be the erasure of mental frontiers and schema, products of those faculties which, in the dismal university of the modern mind, are made perpetually to compete for funds. Poetry as practiced by

Moritz places us between conditions *en route*, like Ulysses in "Ulysses en Route" or the fugitive family in "Rest on the Flight into Egypt" in one of his recent books. As Moritz said in the afterword to the original edition of *Black Orchid*, "Poetry is always shipwreck and gives clear sight."

We can take the measure of the poet's anarchism (and incidentally note the inheritance of those revolutionary precursors) in that same afterword, where he claims that poetry is a dis-ordering of experience, that poetry comes in order to smash order and admit the real, to show that ordered experience has in fact been non-experience, an abstract existence within a schema, a shell.

In relation to the other faculties and disciplines, poetry acts as a kind of conscience, forever calling upon them to resist their tendency to calcify into concepts, or fall into one form or another of technological sleep, and return instead to the task of "probing for reality." That reality is *telos* and not the assumed foundation is a primary article of faith here; reality is what the poem invokes, what it serenades, and what, by the poem's own live presence, is called into being, "incarnating that remote possibility."

It is interesting to see how this plays out in a beautiful poem like "Music and Exile," where the mode is lyric rather than polemic, and the carrying tone one of longing rather than declaration:

> Some say that mine is a work of images
> appearing and ceasing to exist in succession,
> like static and silence on a radio tuned at night
> to some station perhaps beyond its range:
> there is only nothingness to connect the flashes.
> How is it that no one has detected you,
> your voice, the thread of all things seen and heard?
> Is it that you are not an image
> but a ghost, the idea of a melody,
> a cry from beyond the loud wall of the rain?

How does poetry incarnate the "remote possibility" of a reality that exists both beyond and just *there*, close as the radio, distant as that station outside its range? I think that incarnation, that summoning into linguistic materiality, has everything to do with craft, which here involves a sure sense of the tension between the 'sentence' and fall of the prose line and the irresistible lift of lyric, as though the experiences of exile and music named in the title were struggling for control of the poem.

It is no less intriguing to observe how the pervasive musicality of these poems, giving carrying power to their probing insights and equivocal wisdom, is balanced by pure metaphorical pizzazz, with the surprise and sudden humour of discovery. Sometimes the move performs a far reach, close to the surrealism of Péret or Eluard, as in the presentation of the fantasy woman who "coagulates, coming to rest/ like television programs in a bowl/ of wax fruit." On other occasions the figure completes itself with the satisfaction and alarm which accompanies some fresh disclosure of the real, like those children of our middle years, "passenger dolphins/docking in the fountain of youth," or Diana's body, "which men call 'white'" but is really "a nameless colour in which everything relaxes." And then, suddenly, the appearance, in "Northern Spring," of two chaste haiku-like stanzas which seem to summon an entire implied mythology:

> The frogs sing
> to the bones of the reeds
> to put on flesh.
>
> A blackbird, a waiting heart,
> stirs
> in the defrauded ribs.

It is as though that near perfect pitch which Moritz seems to enjoy in musical aspects of the poem, the ear that judges exactly the relation of prose *gravitas* to lyrical lift, had its equivalent in a rheostat controlling the style and extent of its metaphorical reach.

Early Poems, like all of Al Moritz's work, leaves me reassured about the potential efficacy of poetry, of mind engaged with world on all fronts—politically, mythically, psychologically. This is clearly the work of a poet who is not only committed to his vocation, but, one is tempted to say, condemned to it, obliged to follow its rhythms and ambitions rather than his own. And we can only be thankful, surveying this teeming, unpredictable, many-mansioned ark, that he has been so afflicted.

ENRICHING SHADOW:
A. F. MORITZ'S *EARLY POEMS*

John Hollander

A.F. Moritz's long residence in Canada (since 1974) did little for a long time to assure his public prominence among other American poets of his generation. Of his entire oeuvre of some thirteen books of poetry (aside from his translations, criticism, biography and literary history) one, a very fine collection called *The Tradition* (1986), was published in this country, in the highly selective series formerly brought out by Princeton University Press. The present volume, an extremely impressive collection of all his earlier poems up through the 1983 volume, *The Visitation*, brings to readers in the United States a chance to catch up on the first part of a body of work by one of the strongest American poets of his generation.

Throughout his work, Moritz displays a superb poetic technê or mastery of the art of verse, which gives it that quality that we traditionally, albeit a little lamely as well as nostalgically, call an identifiable "voice." He has written interpretively of poets as different as Spenser, Tennyson and Ashbery, and has heard a great deal of their verbal music (as well as that of Byron, Hölderlin and Georg Trakl, whose importance he has himself acknowledged). And yet while his free verse is as different from Ashbery's as it is from Merwin's, or that of the late A.R. Ammons, or Robert Penn Warren's, or Mark Strand's, or Charles Wright's, or any of the wealth of different modes produced by May Swenson's great and fecund formal imagination, it is just as distinctive. But it has been the prophetic moral vision emerging in Moritz's last four or five books that has become dominant for me. A central visionary trope of life among ruins—of civilizations, communities, institutions, artifacts, even verbal and conceptual constructions (and to this degree his concerns are in the tradition of some of Blake and of Goya's etchings)—emerges most explicitly in the volume called *Mahoning* (1994), and his poems generally abound in vivid and complex allegorizations of human sexuality.

My first acquaintance with this important poetry came from having been sent copies of two of his earlier books, both published in Canada. *The Visitation* and *Between the Root and the Flower* (1982) both seemed to me to be remarkable work. I wrote him at the time, explaining that although I was sent dozens of books of verse published by small presses all the time, what I had found in these volumes were real poems, which was quite rare. Shortly thereafter, I had occasion to mention to Harold Bloom that I had been startled by some unusually good poetry emerging from a pile of the usual dismal volumes of indifferent verse; on learning the name of the author, Bloom exclaimed, "Yes, I know his work. He is a true poet" (a term he uses even more sparingly than I do). On telling *this* story, a month or so after, but without mentioning the poet's name, to Mark Strand (a poet with very different tastes from Bloom's), *he* responded by saying, "Is that Al Moritz? He's wonderful." What this meant was partially that without yet achieving any sort of popularity, and while being unknown to journalists of contemporary verse, the great imaginative depth of Moritz's poetry, its real originality, its unusually strong technical resources, had all been perceived, aside from my personal judgment, by two very important writers—a poet and a critic. (The admiration of Moritz's poetry by John Ashbery and W.S. Merwin I only learned of several years later.) Given that I had not known—nor did I then get to know—any of his poems prior to *The Visitation* and *Between the Root and the Flower*, it gives me great pleasure to say a few words about the present volume now.

Prominent in all this early poetry is the enriching shadow—rather than the burdensome or oppressive one—of a legacy from surrealism, both in the generation of images and in some of the larger logical and rhetorical syntactical structures which contain them and shape the individual poems they inhabit. On the other hand, there are the equally prominent more ordinary sorts of syntax of clauses and sentences, a control of tone and movement from higher to more colloquial levels of diction, and the adaptation of expository style to the meditative rhythms of lyric poetry. All of these work to enforce the same kind of counter-balance to various freely associative syntactic modes that Dryden once claimed to be an advantage of rhyme over blank verse, that it "bounds and circumscribes the fancy." Paul Valéry remarked on analogous virtues of any strict prosodic mode. The paratactic accretion of plangent and expressive images—an archaic mode of early modernist "experimentation"—can do little to keep them from floating away from attentive concern. But Moritz's deeply controlled free verse, so attentive to the demands of the ear (as so much dull contemporary free-verse, the later-modern equivalent of Victorian jingle, is not) provides an additional analogue of Dryden's rhyme. From the beginning, these poems propound, even as they are propounded by, an original kind of coherence (as perhaps all poems must). In a poem called "Catalogue of Bourgeois Objects," toward the end of *Black Orchid* (1981), the middle book collected here, images are unbounded and uncircumscribed by any of the grammatical and expository devices of subordination, and one may see in this both a *reductio* and a farewell to some of the internal structures of many of these poems: they are merely concatenated and ordinal.

It was hardly surprising for me to hear, on reading many of the poems in *New Poems* (1974) and *Here* (1975), some rhetorical echoes of John Ashbery, in the kinds of modulation between expository and conversational modes, in the deploying of often wildly figurative predications

framed. But one can also detect early instances of Moritz's originality in a fine little poem called "Addiction," beginning

> I wish we could control this revolting
> want of control: these people
> with their spongy eyes, their mouths
> of trembling shoehorns...

and continuing with a list of mechanical tropes for unloving sexuality. But halfway through the poem, we see the speaker drawing back from the obsessional pit to firmer ground as the poem concludes:

> What if, doing it every day,
> we resemble pistons, and the slow poison
> cuts our lives off at 70:
> it's the grim determination
> of our passion. And beyond this, even I—
> defended in childhood by my strong father
> the piano and my mother the virtuoso
> from knuckles among warehouses—even I
> am addicted to the mild light of words.

Whatever of Ashbery one might still hear in the first lines of this passage, the conclusion, with its moving glimpse of a domestic seminary of poetic vocation, and its invitation to extend the wish to control of the opening to the obsessions of surrealist fancy itself with metamorphic fragments and with the world as a cabinet of erotic curiosities, is quite original. Almost in designed contrast, in this same early volume, is the lovely "Soft Body," a reinvention of the medieval *aubade*. It acknowledges at the outset a traditional ambivalence at the dawn of a new day which signals both the end of night and the necessary departure of the speaker, the male lover: "Morning, outfitted with a pun / for demonstrative sorrow . . ." and in the course of the poem, morning becomes personified, momentarily in the speaker himself, and then in a female body.

Throughout the first two books reprinted here—in such poems as "The Extreme Situation," "Fragment," the title poem of *Here*, "As Formerly," "The Uses of the Past," to select only a very few—we find indications of new directions. But there seems to be a crucial turning-point in *Black Orchid*, in which the reader may find as I did not only a broadening of perspective and a new variety of tones, but another sort of poem as well. "Poem," the sequences of "Northern Spring" and "The Ground," "Pauses," "The Ravine," "Because the Wind Went Over Us," "Stabbing," "The Problem," "Mansions," "Memories of a Small Town Childhood" and "The Underground," for example, all seem to look ahead into poetic distances that Moritz's subsequent work continues to explore, profoundly and, for the grateful reader, always rewardingly. Even without his subsequent books, these poems would signal an unusual talent, sensibility, poetic power and capacity for growth. In the light of them, this powerful volume remains all the more valuable.

New Poems

THINKING ABOUT DREAMING

Suddenly the hammock wraps me up,
a new cocoon. The daiquiri approaches
twirling her spear
to enlist me in her troop of cars.

"Chrysalid of vengeance," says someone else.
Indeed, I am as enchanted
as the elements in a ticking bomb.

Every day my father shines his lamp
over the links of the chain,
a warder fingering bones on the floor.
It is all so clear, how the old ones are estranged.
I follow him. He puts on his white smock
and opens me up. Who knows what I was
before he showed me how a rope
strings a bunch of cans together?

The men are marching furiously, flies
upside down on the ceiling of the womb.
The patient women sleep like the flowering
of a shell thrusting a hole into a wall.

The old schoolteacher with her penis in hand
points out the light. Really, no one can wait
for the dark to come round again.

The moon will be bathing down in the wet woods.
I think I'll leave my hounds at home.
I think I'll go out to her and kiss her
and enter her as a fish thrown back.

A WOMAN

A woman also is a verb
like everyone of all the useless
lumps later than ever again.
She appears gun in hand like
an imitation and bang! mountains of fat
make up a little of what the sea wears away.
Everything is as still as traffic,

airliners, the routines of conglomerates,
girls on the make, those pulp statues
of bad men with cement feet
signaling plaintively to hulls in harbor.
In the motionlessness of violet dusk
she coagulates, coming to rest
like television programs in a bowl
of wax fruit. Her solidity
appeared one night in the semblance of a plum
and the eater found matter in it
for a dream: his mother
was a stone chorus girl and on
the oval of her belly he triumphed
in the bicycle races, just as she always wanted.
Do you remember, though, that boy
on the bench, arms raised
as if tied by piano wire to the trees?
That just then she started to glow a little
like the soul leaving a stone?
How sitting there beside him among the poor
lights of the sky and ocean
she kissed his nipple as if hungry again?

The Choice

His back to radiance, besieged
by chuckling radiators, the release
of sexual tension was his only choice.
Ah, but in a world beyond high tension
there would be no wires of any kind.
This is not to imply telepathy,
which is merely being a rock when rock
is not what you are, alias nirvana,
alias television, alias pornographic moment.
No, it means conversation:
everyone having to talk to you
to get farther than falling from the tree
with a soft thud that attracts a nearby squirrel.
Everywhere now the pyramids of young trees
are complicating more peculiar droplets
of interlacing viewpoint, like heads
planning festoons of comparison.
The separability of heat and light

throws off its gown—which, it turns out,
was also the castle wall—and drifts
slowly down the moat now a river
like a girl who surfaced an instant
to deliver you this naked gift:
your sister and her own. What a soft
carpet are all these erstwhile spears!
A clump of bushes, a pile of leaves
suggest you two add yourselves
to the general volubility:
the endless ejaculation of a marriage.

ADDICTION

I wish we could control this revolting
want of control: these people
with their spongy eyes, their mouths
of trembling shoehorns, billhooks for penises
and bear traps for vulvas.
One taste of sunlight and at once
they can't do without it. Water,
the same, and food, and air,
and a dozen other squalid habits.
Some—like their copulation,
a rusting carnation in a cut-glass neck—
are not physically compulsive but
the partners can't stop wanting them to be:
so we desire to be raped
by love, who would fill us, they say,
with an oil from the lit braziers of stars.
What if, doing it every day,
we resemble pistons, and the slow poison
cuts our lives off at 70:
it's the grim determination
of our passion. And beyond this, even I—
defended in childhood by my strong father
the piano and my mother the virtuoso
from knuckles among warehouses—even I
am addicted to the mild light of words.

The Hollow Wards

Not like a coffin of lenses in the airport.
More like a beautiful tinsel chandelier.
"All the pieces of my face!" you screamed.
"Am I everything or do I just look that way?"
So Evening, my girl in green, slim
as a panorama, afraid of her hips' intentions,
has undressed and stares at the mirror which
hangs at the center of her body
like a drop of water. In philosophical mood
she says, "I am the imaginative reflections
of this drop," and the sickness in her breasts
flies to her hand, a gun butt.
That's when they spotted the absent puppeteer
with his nooses perched on the chandelier.
The frenzied cadaver himself in the telescope
sucked at all the flying sights
like someone breathing under tons of sand.
Even and perhaps especially in the Great Fetid Age
ice covers both poles, where, we suspect,
are the traps of Inner Earth. Their purpose is
they are open to anything at all.
A profitable enterprise would be
import some persons into these hollow wards.

In Reality

In reality is talking about singing
but it comes out how nothing but sex and death
in a fishbowl with sunrise back of it
prods the tin cans, "Become beautiful, dear,
take the feedbag off your horse."

Even this was held in the air of a hidden flute
with someone's footsteps going alone after it
down the cliff into the fleshly white stone landscape.

Now an impregnable bubble has encased the composition
and it is only here that happy pilots
enter the body of the sea
with fatal speed
as if it were the end of the world.

Sweet Outrage

Together on the lowest steps we talked
through never-ending midnight while the stairwell
repealed our voices. View from the blue cliff.
For sleep there was the snoring thunderbird
in your toolshed and your tunnel vision:

how you lost me once the September wind
had detached me from my thistle. Which was long
before we could believe the strange report
of pears, knit firmly as wine, shaped like
the hollow of a large and a small mouth kissing.

So I went up to the attic to watch out
for anything coming. And you returned
to carrying cupfuls of earth from the foundation.
But every night the warden mixed new mortar
in your tear ducts, which are my veins.

And so we laughed: wooden chisel, flying machine,
a long dive into the phosphorescent sea...
and nevertheless you in the Mediterranean night courtyard
and flowers sucking on numerical stone:
the sweet outrage of the sundial by sleep.

She Speaks

More frightening than the sky itself.
Who knows where in all that nudity
it hides its sex? You expect it
in the center of the ceiling between the mirrors
like a symmetrical cascade of chandelier.
If that's a fig leaf, it's on fire:
someone must have discarded a match
in the little valley of black question marks.
Just in case, from now on I'm wearing clothes
when I go outside. We'd better sew
an asbestos lining into the earth's bikini.
And now where will the rain come from?
I think I will make my home under
a he-goat's tail. There this imposter sky
with its third eye but minus the other two

will never see me. I'll be happy.
Each morning I will put up my shutter
and appear like a little pink chipmunk
shaking my duster from my hole
into the urinary brook beneath.
When that is all done, how great
my reward will be, like swallowing a balloon
hydrogen mercilessly inflates
toward the breaking point. Just like
a sharpened log roasted in the fire,
we will rush into the sun, maybe,
and leave it bleeding
and I will be out of here.

DIFFERENCE OF OPINION

How firmly, like a complicated flower
as slowly moving, as apparently unmoved
in the moment beyond apogee
as in the bud, you entered
that white room where all the news
was of old age in Florida, on your arm
the bridegroom tall and liquid,
already stiff and silver as a flute.

For me it was different if much the same.
I thought of the strange water
Florida might have held
before it was built over. The ground,
which a man is said to "spurn beneath his feet,"
seemed as gray that summer
as our fathers' skins when they quit wanting life.
Did you empty your place beside me
because of my fantasy, that ice
is a flower too, snow the pollen of the sky,
the year merely a word, the so-called spring
only one further hour
of the continually advancing season?

We too are terrified of living
beyond our time, out into the burning
of a surprise in which no one imagines
any peace. The flute's tone

between a russet sky and the gravid rocks
remains the same as slowly it corrodes,
but though you expect and play it, is this music
that remembers itself in brittle reeds
any stiller because mournful? We fear most
the approaching peace of the rivers
simply frozen at one more end of things.

Like Water

Already when the furred solidity of peaches
first meant to you a physical desire
that had no outlet, the former things
had overcome you. Only you
felt the age in the blank translucence
of those billion pebbles rubbed and whispered to
constantly by a weak surge.

And though I wanted to make plans for you
and spoke in your ear, the words were like the water
that you knew not as an emblem
of eternity but as the thing itself:
tired, desperately unable to die,
softening space to a silver mirror,
already as old as you will have to be.

In Winter

The swirling tire ruts in the mud
of the field outside our window: these
seemed to us emblems of the road
we thought we had been looking for and found
smashed like a rusted spring. The spring

is coming, will turn to a dawn-colored
broth these brittle sculptures
the motorcycles left us a sign
for our conversion. You looked across
to the trees. If you are caught, it isn't

within walls, behind windows, in the flesh.
It's in this seeing that already finds

beyond this another winter, where
the changes, though noticeable, are not
of the slightest importance to anyone.

THE FIRST CHAPTERS OF GENESIS

No more my neighborhood the crushed
cathedral. Disappointed men,
where are you today with all your arms
that used to make one pitiful gesture, raising
and shaking shredded fingers
to imitate a head? No more
puffed and drained fragments of human
bodies roll over, at last turning
pink and yellow near the black
lipstick of a simple smile.

This feeling of self-possession,
awareness of a hand in its glove.
These bodies bounding in transparent globes.
When did I move to this room
empty and full of light
and in a deep angle
a mirror hung opposite a window?

So the prince spoke, puzzled,
on the eminence from which in former days
nothing had been visible but dead
airplanes and burst balloons
lying wrecked all over night.

Thus the warrior mettle awakens
at the end of a season
of knowing everything.
His distraught father saw him appear suddenly
in the surrounding air, which served
as tongue to touch the glowing limit
of his body: O sleepers on your couch,
it was saying, and you sleepless wanderers
in forest and hardware store,
assemble. And a rush began to gather
out of here and into the brown fields.

Cab

Considering the deaths of fantastic graces
such as garish leaves scaffolded
on the rays of stone lamps,
our cab turned upward at the wilderness road.

These are strange little people here, leaning
under green awnings of woven hair
in front of an empty turquoise storefront,
with their disorderly boxes full of seeds
and nickels. They're so short, their legs,
for they must have legs, are pushed
no doubt through invisible holes
in the floor of existence, the feet
dangling somewhere else in clear water.

There a tiny fountain spits without pause,
like the harmony the baking noise of a battlefield
comes down to in moonlight.

Tap on the glass, dear. Driver,
return where you don't understand me.
As a matter of fact the blade of my letter opener
was growing fuller there, the sap or something
else rising, and soon the word would be rose.

Soft Body

Morning, outfitted with a pun
for demonstrative sorrow,
you become me as falling inward
asleep from the heartfelt pounding of
a blank expression covering the window looking in
you turn to a momentary failure
to see this scene, as beautiful as immense.

Now the flight gropes, the mouth
open to spew is desperate to swallow.
I fell here to avoid the touch of wind,
glances of stars on my shoulders; now I find
arms hugging the curvature of earth,
breast and landscape married

along a glowing line, a head submerged
and drinking the green light that changes in ocean.

The embrace puts on huge garments of being viewed,
one above the other. At the center of an eye
opening on itself, we feel the first
finger of its surprise as the break of ground
towards blueprints all night thrashed out.

These affairs fall on her and me from the way
day returns and the eyes start seeing things,
a matter of freedom as a sheet,
the problem of what to make
of woman, lax entrée
to the immobile gate of bone. Still, soft
body of morning, I'm going out
into you, you to return me
a hard light in the afternoon.

They're Tearing Down the Walls Again Upstairs

We are materialists and yet salvation
remains something more than salvage, something
like the first instant of a movement unlike
its motive: the way a ballad comes from the pure
accident of angry people meeting.

Let me out, she shrieks, thumping on the door,
my heart with her party hat on and dress pulled up
where I left it, hiding her face from her wet thighs.
Annoyed, I sit in my study inflating balloons,
each one improved with a different map of that face.

Out of desperation we two end up going
for a walk, like a little girl in red with a blue
face following her on a string. There are
strange things now in the progressively calmer air,
there are the ghosts of seeing everything.

Blind Girl

How is the blind girl come here,
deaf, without touch or taste or scent,
voiceless,
closed husk in a night of fog?

Beautiful as a sunken city,
you make water from our ignorance.

You are not one of those theaters an audience creates:
your body is grave, no news escapes it.

And when, awakening, the lightning stretches out
its liquid wire of manganese,
there are no earth and sky to form
the gap it needs to leap, no wall in which
the new light could be fissure.

Suddenly the vision of you is as good as dream.

We move at once to the hotel of brick windows.
Here the social activity is intense
and at seldom night the bored nerves of our eyes
amuse themselves as formerly,
assembling things like you on the empty dark.

A Graceful Permission

A graceful permission was your child
under the live oaks within sandstone walls,
a white patch on a little rock the sun.
We feel outward from your deeper temperature,
its slow motion, its hue of shaded water.

What good is it outside there,
our dinner sucked up before it escapes earth
by the stiff siphon of daylight
into the summer deep freeze and the oven winter?

There we are totally an idiot,
the blessedness of losing fingers to the cats of night,
beforested in the old wive's tale of night,
a quadriplegic in its armless hug.

And there we bleed pure white, let loose in night's
blank eyelid, inditing the wisdom of the tribe.

Here is the sobbing garden hemmed with salt.
Seen from the water of night,
the far-off dunes are cool and deep.
We drink of the blue well flecked with white of the drought.

There is more here than can be known, enough
to occupy us forever. Our eyes turn inward,
from the smoked window the tattoo is broadcast
while the sun lunges at the ruby door.

He Would Have Coursed the Doe

He would have coursed the doe across her body
but that night gave out on the frayed tapestry,
the knight whose horse had raised one foreleg
on the bridge fading over the stream,
the hunter with arrows sheathed and bow rigidly
dangling as he looks back to castle walls.
And the wary doe looks back far-off
along her body from the edge of a white pool.
Though the hills, the fields at harvest,
the silver entangled woods are flat,
his eyes of yarn won't see her
where she listens paused to drink.

Always on the Verge

Hand closed too tightly on the liquor
held in a cheap eggshell, the fire leaped out,
exacerbated by broken bells. O fondly remembered
sutured smile, the mountains sway and waver,

the sun being visible at last and seen
for itself: an axe, saying: Bring me the limbs
of the child. And certainly this sun is a form attacking
with a certain grace an idled lake that lies
in the suck and gargle conveyed to us
on the yellow shaft falling from the bathroom door.

The whole landscape is the coal where flames of water
waver in the wind, a sheet filling with a body,
why fire they say became man:
to intensify, to become freer and more random—
mere conjectures, based firmly on
the crescent tin can structure that split you from within
but is only a blinding sliver of vapor on reaching the air.

And though you throw your hooks after it,
they are clumsy as arms. One untrimmed fingernail
by chance draws blood from the breast
of the flower bed, which excites him—he begins
to lick you, he's seen a photograph of you
clad only in phonograph records, knees
open and a long whistling scream
coming from your mouth as rapid motion
crams oxygen into your vulva. Yes, your kite
has always had a tail which hovering high
it consumes slowly with relish
to the point of disastrous dizziness.

The Extreme Situation

The wild man had committed a violin
and went on in his teeth, which were after all
the gift of nature, to soap a million, never
giving them a chance. Nothing but soap:
imagine the horror of it, to be trapped
in a small room with a soap maniac,
knowing there's no escape,
gradually ceasing to care or even to notice.

The toaster said, that sodden banquet,
"Yea, verily, I say unto," and quickly
I switched it off, recognizing the preamble to the news.
More interesting perhaps that these cowboy signals,
these doctor and detective signals, mingled with briefer
but more intense signals as to the shame
of menstruation and so on exist in the air around here,
though you don't know it, indelibly marking your spleen.

As you confessed, you are
constantly distracted by the sound this makes,

not in itself, which is merely a silent nervousness,
but in you, a lot of echoes
you never think of mentioning to anyone.

Automatically it occurs, as
the lost control of the bladder, the lost sense of time,
the roach unknown to science supernaturally slow
in its progress up the spine, where it can't be reached
except by X-rays, intravenous feedings, oxygen tents,

and I never wanted to have my faith
tested by other means than the meat grinder
applied to the arm, the burning bamboo splinter,
the white room closed for years and years.

But to be sneezed on by forgetfulness,
the way a road rises one morning in the sun's place
over the eastern rim of the rose garden…
Indeed, I never saw a rose garden, come to think,
they were all gyroscopes.

What good is any but the extreme situation?

Relief Is at Hand

A multifaceted eye sees you
as diffused amber and a threat.

A blowtorch bends closer to the shape
in lipstick appearing on my bony cheek.

This room no longer the size of breathing,
this dreaming no longer dying,

and the hot sweat that lubricates
my body's midst, the smooth moon

split in half, and the black cowl
peering from rocks: who could sleep now?

I want to rest awhile
in view of this parade and this warning.

Fragment

Unrescued water in its dish,
the sea thrusts up a flat chest
to parallel the sky, wrinkles and crawls
with its impossible longing to fall apart
and outward in imitation of what covers.
We, dear, are familiar with this place
and the hatred of it. Chiefly of that water
thickened with a little dirt, you were
the perfect lure and cell with which to cut
a small part of the sun's heat and hold it,
perpetual mourning, in the shape called "man."

Here we were forced to live, there being
no space in our house, remember? It
had filled up with the sound of doors closing,
and you had learned your constant gesture there,
passing a hand across your forehead to wipe away
the sense of a web. Your hand
crosses your face like darkness over a moon
and then we watch it slowly coming back,
always fearing some difference, always
reassured. How can it change?
From its first renewal it has held all age,
unlike a man's face, like any woman's
where the ancestors' countenance grows plain
and the terror of death is relieved
in a boy's finding he is no other cancer
than the alternation of the days and nights.

Your gesture made of you that moon
who rules by day equally with the sun,
moon white and soiled, a hole in the umbrella sky:
the gray arrows that space was shivered to
fell on us, turning silver in the sun,
and our bodies streamed, parts like water on stone,
parts like water on leaves and trunks of trees,
parts like water on more delicate plants.
If we were crying then, the rain was the only tears,
and I saw the tracks of rain in the dusty air,
they were hollow stems and through them empty heaven
sucked up earth to flower elsewhere,
breathing itself downward until we stood
on a balloon inflated with vacuum.

I describe here the outward romance of childhood
only to help explain your discovery
of that infinite, elemental world you'd hidden
and forgotten in a spaceless room. Remember?
The tall man and woman dreamed of walls cracking
and our four eyes lost
when the string around mother's neck drawn through
every pupil on earth tore and sent them
careering crazily on the flat floor?
And in panic sleeping, father hugged my knees
as the house dwindled away,
slipping into unstoppable holes lost somewhere
in its own corners. Such were our heads,
placed among things as islands more real than they
and holding the mouths of caves whose entrails
are a new earth that has swallowed this one.

And even this little in those days
was only suspected, meant no more to us
than a hint in the direction of nothing:
flashes of bored nerves on the empty dark,
from which the mind made histories.
We were as yet still in that second shell,
the cramping chamber of the unwilling martyr
who feels himself beginning to grow so big
he splits his place and limps off
through the rubble of the city of gnomes:
a huge man
deformed by his birth to the likeness of a bird.

The Fruits of Contemplation

The body of the ocean with
genitalia of water evaporating
engenders a prospectus of cancer
in his lover far away:
                    "What
behemoth like a rising cyst
puts its back up in the belovèd
skin cut by my ships? And that
new island with its central hole,
belching into the open bag of blue

as foully as a hospital: down in it
is the brown polyp of a heart
boiling like stew, its thick rind
exploded continually by bubbles and dire
borborygmi.
                Yet the sea still rains
over me and in dirty rivers
of my sweat and his excess my makeup
runs down to him. I will expose
all my surface, exterior
and interior alike, and moisten
every part of me, lest in
the vibration of this heat my eyes
fall into me like fragments
of the broken sun.
                Again
the clouds drift over me, far inland
my eyes turn green in the shadow,
the ground smooth, the quincunxial
vegetation like a clipped park. Not even
the seabirds know it, perched
on my fingernails, if you are
dead as the acid-eaten staring
fish you wash up constantly
into my palms' pink basins."

A Prison Diary

From the foundation
all night long the whimsical warden
kept us prisoners awake
with a rhythmic pounding on the pipes.
I remember what fear there was
when I embraced my wife: fear
that filled the cell with the frenzy
of fifty clocks, for all our years
together made fifty at that time.
I remember how each dawn cut out
the old skyline of the yard:
the broken inverted eggshell over us
would gray, then fester to whiter light
and this brought out the forms, like bones

piled by chance the way clouds
suggest a human use: a tall
guillotine shaped like the letter A;
a gibbet with its dangling noose,
which seemed in imaginative moments
like a harness for a bird; a boiling
pot with its red emanation; and in
the background the cross against the sky.

Here

I   HERE

We are as young in sunlight as the stones
that will live almost forever, we are as old
in shadow as the stones that have had to wait
almost since the beginning. Amber lights
open from time to time in a mask of cloud.
Between are brown moments in the coal-dust air.
To cease is not permitted here.
To complete something is not permitted.
Out of the river climb elongated musics,
oddly shaped shrieks of light,
walls of brittle, unmortared bricks.
Staring littered and sunken in the hard
mud of the banks, the third eyes are glass.

TODAY

The woman who hallowed distances in my eyes
looked at her wristwatch on the cliff's edge: dusk,
and the storm of tragic flaws was freezing around her,
gemming the statue and its sparrow caged
in the pyramided fingers of bronze hands.

A black garden. The waters cringe, a man
basks in darkness, nervous body leaves.
To rest, far from the sunburnt clearing
where limbs and head and sex attack the torso:
this is the ideal of the specter.
It rains,
the piecemeal illusions quake and stumble.
If grass stirs, the roots of the hair stir.
A cloud covers the moon, the eye closes.
Soft confusion shakes a mildewed cloth.

It seems a battle tortures gears in the sky,
a muffled music grinds, waters are falling,
wrestling in cisterns. Out of distance now
bright pearl the hand of the giantess comes back,
with two long fingers walking on the path.
Its head, its severed wrist, drinks from a cloud,
the slit in the palm bleeds day.

Betrayed Light

Her coming had been sunrise. The star of figures
appeared and settled above her head,
its golden band sheaving her blows of light
into a day of numbered staves. What love
demands this pillory, this song of what will happen,
of how the single character says goodbye
and the knife parts him? The song is of divorce
although in fact the memory of our marriage
is only a pain incited by her turned back
and betrayed light piercing sullen water.

The Art of Poetry

The alarming radio of morning spoke
of eastern wars. But the same voice, changed,
came also from a blue tulip by the bed
with news of a wanderer underground.
So dreams died. How could we sleep again,
be scissors closing to cut
the flower of intellect from the images?
A new light was changing the kinds of space.
Walls that had hovered in darkness set themselves
and whitened like clay baking. The chandelier
appeared in the watery round mirror,
its featureless three bulbs glowing within
the halo of gold foil. The curtains moved,
cascade of roses under a light warm wind,
and in the spreading clearness
all was deformed from what it clearly is—
the faint clashing
of curtain hooks was the music of deformity.
Just as a man who stoops down in the street
may be made, struck by the sun, a headless knot
where all that tends to death convenes,
then he stands up again
in glory, human and common—
so dawn read for a moment
the lost allegory of our room.

Soliloquy of a Dreamer Absent from His Dream

Long ago the universe set within me
and at once in front of a rising sun
two birds collided and fell dead.
Now from the gap in the double mountain
of their bodies at every dawn and twilight
women walk down a plank of sun or moonlight
through the window of this cell into my eyes.
My thought is not the question: sealed,
it sits forgotten in a bottle. No:
I hear those women
like Rumor or some kinder goddess
walking softly on the roof of my mouth.
Over the shingles under the hard
dome of the sun-exhausted sky
they wander, enduring their jars
of water that chastens fire to words,
seeking a way to enter or to leave.

A Disease of the Throat

There is a man rasping like a blade.
The spear of all his grandmothers is piercing
his throat slowly from its ambush in the trees.
When it is finished, the bearers will take him up
on that spit and carry him
to be disassembled in the warehouse:
and they will eat the pieces again
before his time, those flowers the grandfathers.

If ever I wake up he is singing to me,
music as soft as being forced
at knife point from this green cliff
and falling upward to be crushed
or drowned or smothered in the sky.
His face is the pale daylight feather
of a moon dropping over my shoulder
as I record. "Hurry and finish," he says.
"That won't be any use to you when I'm gone."

At the City Dump

A heart more morbid than a silver flute
in a forest of saxophones, consenting to die
of sleep in the snow of its own voice:
such was I in the noisy days I spent
mute on the sunstruck porches of your ear.

Now I empty these unused cans of music
from my frayed pack of adolescence into the river
that dumps its acid in the sea.

From far away the observer thinks he watches
a waterfall of metal restored at last
to primeval fluidity.
As the angry water eats the idiot husks
and the songs escape, an aetherial concert
as of bursting bubbles brings him,
almost inaudibly,
reassurance of the heavenly city.

And he seems to see a huge bird rearising
in the sooty smoke of the nearby landfill,
touched now by the fiery baton of morning.

The Destinies of Water

As at the approach of a razor,
whistling spaces
sag loosely in gray air. A dry
tree's reminiscences of hair
low upon the forehead
in the foreground obscure the prospect.
The sky's brittle smile
stretches like tinted enamel now
over the late west: already,
bursting its symbols, being
is revealing itself, Don Juan
retires for the night and on the sill
his teeth of a rainbow
await the bitter sleet to be cleansed.

And where an early summer evening
extends tentacles from the river bank
come scents of the reeds and peach trees, darkness
indistinguishable from mist or tired eyes,
gauze like a web deepening the cocoons
around adolescent forms.

In the dim park the idea for a basin
cracks unseen, to the stream seeps away
an instinct to desire the strength
that might have borne all the destinies of water.

THE OLD MAN

Try to recall the day, not long ago,
when the old man came to stay with you.

In the instant when his face, like that of Thais,
surprised you in the desert city,
you felt the talons of his withered legs
grapple your throat and shoulders.

He took down the morning from its perch
and put it with palpitations of the heart,
homeless noises, wandering fragments of light.

The day was a rocky beach
where part of a message is arranged,
and in a cave a skeleton.

By noon he was a slow cancer
indistinguishable from life.

Now, carrying a young peach tree,
you don't pause to notice
his shadow lengthen
where he stands, a statue in the garden.

THE DEAD

Now that you dead forget the boundary
between yourselves and us, knock on our doors,
litter garbage over our lawns, over our beds,

fill the air with words as hard as gravel
pelting into the house, I'm forced to ask you,

Undo my sin. Fathers, I have prayed
to believe in death, that the living are alone,
and relegate your misery to the ground.
When I thought I was dying, I said it is
a single man who passes, like one year.

If I hug and crush your shadows now, will that
force blood again to ooze in the white veins?
If I set my back against the irreverent earth
that rolls ever farther from you, will you
dethrone the lizard, lord of the quick today?

In the Well-Clipped Meadow

In the well-clipped meadow the dead and living
grew indistinguishable at twilight,
when someone can appear or leave unnoticed
with the changing colors of the air.

Their words were soft darkened coals,
downy ashes gliding on small wings,
whistling above the lawn.
Their king's huge crown sat on the faceless mountain peak.

And they were destined to be smaller and grayer
than blades of grass. The dream itself we saw
slinking away, going down toward the two trees
that formed for us the gate to the night woods.

II   As Formerly

Much to the coroner's amazement,
your body opened its eyes at sunrise.
Just when we had gathered to hear the
cause of our deliverance, the whip
was coiling again. We saw it all,
the long hours in the treeless
brickyards and for nothing: to replace
the houses the spring rains washed
into the river—the rains

that water the corn that keeps us
alive enough to need the houses.
We remember what you told us yesterday
and the day before: that a spring day
reminds you of spring, a gray low-ceilinged one
of gray days, and a big blue noon
galvanizes all your big blue emotions.
We are long familiar with your boat fantasy:
going down to the landing, the luxurious
fittings, the supposed variety of the banks
and finally the ocean, with no account
taken of food, sanitary matters or sleep.
The sun through the willow's lowest leaves
always evokes it. Impossible
to repeat anything perfectly and so
you change it from day to day: you call
this process science. Your face tonight
a little more deathly tells us nothing about
which will be the unique closing of eyes.
It can come at any moment and meanwhile
each morning animates the collection
as an actor puts on his clothes again.

THE USES OF THE PAST

In the beginning is a light cloud floating
through an open door that stands there
in the middle of nowhere. The hill accepts the vapor.
And all at once everywhere something was
forging without perceptible aim
through the golden meadow
to the various ends of earth.
So the evolution of desire
extends its precious pile of mute bearings
to the circular motive
of unanchored colonies of weeds living on air.
In a sense we had been turned to nothing, in a sense
snatched from the path of those hard lights
that come rushing out of mist and disappear,
leaving only a smashed body on the sidewalk.
Now there is a motion in the air, a fear,
the sense of something missed and missed again.

And so with all its baggage, its maimed gestures,
on the balcony in the dim distance
the soul tenderly emerges
from the rumor it has been so many years.
Of humble origins, it turns to do something
for the residue camped below in the muddy field.
A phosphorescence from this moment draws itself up.
The black surface swallows a shining bolus
meteorically altering unruffled night.
Now what can anyone see up there but a dwarf
bursting from the empty ghost of his form?

Words to the Giantess

From this locked room, the scene your old idea
stages again outside my window
to hide your blinding bony palm
is all I can hope to see.
But even in the bogus flesh of leaves
I feel what power is yours: again
your garden blooms savagely despite
how intent it is on last year's conversation,
jokes a little staler, a little more decayed
toward sad philosophy by the teller's
forgetful errors. Again the light and heat
build slowly to excess and topple
more slowly than a wave of dust on the moon.
It doesn't seem to matter to you at all
that change is the essence of your sloth.
"My watch will stop," you boasted, "only
when motion stops." And meanwhile
the extent of your agonizing calm
is an edifice far beyond the scope
of this mortal eye that passes
most quickly of all quick beings
on the bleached, smiling horizon.
Possessed of time for everything that may be,
you are reluctant to acknowledge
the mad day of our childhood: it was merely
a thought better let alone.
Eagerness is for those foolish others
who have grown from your side and claim
to love their passing on and not returning.

You merely wait, content in your regular
cycles of glee and depression,
for what wonders may befall. Maybe they will.
But you, love, disbelieve, despite
your witty heart. One day, you know,
the bitter point of view of these words
will be marked only by a husk on a window sill.
And the remnant still living in that time
will see in it nothing new, though skulls may gape.

LIFE OF DETERMINATION

Once wandering people of excremental sorrow
in these valleys winding out of mists
into watery days...behind them
the mazy river of their progress
is pocked with highlights by the permanent
sunset. They play a music
too regular to hear. They listen
instead to the birds, and their daughters
add syllables, addressing the conchlike ear
of whirlpool or wind devil: "Mother
taught me my name, 'Womb,'
though for many years I understood
this word to be 'Wound.' And now
you tell me my ever regenerated
decay is health and beauty, now
that I can't remember
if you were the fatal knife or became one
in answer to this hole filled with blood."
And always at these pleas of faithless love,
their distant husbands are terrified:
the landscape will blow away!
The husbands modify their sullen rush
to a sullen stillness, make themselves stone
to weight earth down and anchor it
and the fires, imprisoned, grow angry
at the first shock, and then cooler.
Thus wastes solidify, society
(the alternative of nature) becomes complex
and satisfying, and no longer
is felt the humiliating need
to leave the filthy camps behind

for the legend of cleanliness.
They have made virtue from necessity,
inventing a history, erecting towers
to guard their soft wives
from the outlaw brother, Cain or Proteus,
he who comes to the wall all summer
in the forms of every bird, assaulting the blood
with a changeless infinity of calls.
How he probes them with his contentment—
the one thing needful in the birdlike
determination of this life, sexual spring,
huddle of silent feathers under snow.

DIASPORA

In the season of mudslides, the eye,
which had remained alone atop the hill,
saw a broken wrist and three nervous fingers
ooze away in a clump of floating weeds.
A veined red glow just under
the surface of the yellow slime to northward
suggested to it a brother eye
dragged downward by a suffocating head.
Nearby, a forearm rolled continuously
and a buttock was heaving
beside the carcass of a whale. A human
body was dissolved in the disaster,
the drowned brain would have said, adding
that by a prodigious effort of self-love
one might still assemble the world.

THE FAILED DISASTER

Quite expectedly his friends continued
dropping in on him at the prearranged times
in the form of his wife dying, his boy run over
and news that the strangler got his daughter.
His lights burned late that night after they left,
and to the worried neighbors it seemed
that nothing was happening. He was writing,
"Being of sound mind and body, I leave
my perpetually diminishing wino

in the aura and long vista of the streetlamps,
that everyone may at least have something to look at
as far on into the future as we see."
With hopeless distraction he lay
the black barrel gently in his mouth,
a faithless one, willing to brave his ignorance
of man: does he snore in his sleep,
and does he awake next morning, the radio
fighting the familiar birds in his ear?

And we heard it, the horrible
explosion that echoed through the neighborhood
like the evening star come out again. Remember,
from the bathroom you called to me in disappointment,
"I thought that this one had had enough.
I thought that so much misery
might have created not the same old thing,
mere death, but something unexpected:
the man who would barge in here and drain
this soapy water off and lift me
to the brutal openness of a higher plane."

Desert Lament

I can't stand you since the truce line faded out
between your hands and the air, since women
without a thought began erecting temples
of limestone in the wooded clefts of your feet.

Are you trying to steal the fruit of my dehydration,
my fountain sculpture thought—a mass of water
composing the body of a young man
with head and hands and sex of nervous foam?

I asked for some water for my dying wife.
Did you have to reveal to her the sky's endless lake?
That we live in you, more animated than life itself,
a tiny village in the carpenter's palm?

In your aftermath, how stupid the whistling lights,
the brilliance of glass breaking in darkness, odors
blooming eerily in the wall of the pit. How lost to me
are all and nothing, revelations of the senseless night.

The view I must take is fear: we're suspended now
over the seething travail of gathered apples
with no wisdom, no ascent—only our wives
drinking amber at the shaded stream of your eye.

THE GREAT CAPTAIN

"A convenient ray of salt," barked the captain,
and his load of it watching from every blind
fell, fertilizing the hopes of a smashed egg
the blue sky had laid in a nest of severed neck.

Into his piercing white fish the captain loaded fear.
The headache of waiting while it rains
he folded over the vulva in his bed
in the center of his white room. His batman
came to me with snaky broom hair flailing
to blast the spider from my dusty jacket:
the spider who was to be
the seed pearl of my future sojourn
in a truer world.

              Those days I felt so exiled
from the beauty of women, scorched there
among their mothers. If any shadow blessed,
it was a girl who bent above a table
and so became a willow, her hair
lightly brushing the breasts of her reflection.
She was a sign: the earth had grown so thin
under the scraping of the captain and his mothers,
for a moment life shone through it.
And convulsive schools of white fish sailed
for the threatened breach, borne of the spider
far past the continence of dying, which lends
such melancholy music to rendezvous
in old hotels by the sea.

Now the captain dances, armed, his ordnance
(fecal and of infinite weight)
infiltrates the heavenly deserted city.
Till the end of time and after, the dying man
watches aimless spiders on the ceiling,
hears green explosions grow,
marry, give birth, age, die and so on.

Pavement crumbles under the faded palms.
At the deathbed his wife, already united forever
against sterility with his providential ghost,
sobs with him as green words
break up the stones of his eyes.

Genital Obstruction

The mock businessman comes to earth among us,
boarding the bus, whose foggy windows are
his movie every morning. It's a breath of
the exotic to us, the perfume of rotten pears
that escapes slowly from his lap
where the expressionless attaché case reclines.
Milky eyes, the angles of his twitching neck,
remind us of the stretched African dogs
waiting at twilight beyond the huts.
He utters sharp little barks: he has found food
in the last year's *Wall Street Journal* he's always reading.
But his cries, horrible to men, don't scare
the big cats off his kill: a little girl
in a plastic bag in the fields.

Symphonic

Eulalie has the gentle featureless head of a young onion—or of a Van de Graaf generator, for the beauty of her hair springs at surrounding eyes with the stiff irritation of static.

Eunice and Rosalis, when first they catch one another's notice, are camping together where steep meadow merges into mountain. Now they are interested only in being alone.

Cecily and her sisters stand around the house as sentinels, their sharp faces and sharper fingers pointed outward. But in fact they're little more than the tongues with which the storm moans.

Penelope meditates on blood oozing from the living stone beneath her sculptor's chisel, and all the while she is frosting her cake of soap.

Young ladies are natural vandals. In sacking the city, they model their behavior on that of Time: the penises of statues are the first things to go.

And Mercury, about fourteen, stands at the center of a wavy cistern in the angle of a hedge. The sunny freedom, the homosexual omnivalence of his face, is somehow reflected in the strength of his elegant droop, harder than any living man's passion.

But he too will succumb to fate and his pride become an empty socket. Ah, here even now is the novice Hortensia, a mallet lovingly concealed in her barren bloomers.

If only there were some way out of this violent egg-shaped ferment, some stirring under the fossil shell.

If only with a white flash a baton would rise and command preliminary silence in this confusion of gibbering leaves.

The charming narrow-chested skeletons put on flesh, the crumbled fountains of the earth recall their members.

Dawn sound in the orchestra of their conversation.

And over them only the brief night of rest and refreshment ever fall.

THE IMPRINT

When lenses first settled in our bony heads,
we played at being the horses that we saw,
unable to face each other during love.
In the bitch and dog, our later study,
was the intriguing custom of following
the smells of earth. And soon the marvels
of every animal lay sliced
on our plate among familiar greens.

Then your voice flowered from an empty vase:
"There's a certain way of doing things,
which our stars will always describe."
Indeed, you have four dresses and replace them
with new ones much the same.
And if you are growing older or impatient,
it is too slowly to see—although each death
grinds the glass finer, focuses other planes.

Now in bright mist the shining slugs
come out to probe the fingers of a glove,
immense and limp, that has fallen over our ground.
Or not a glove: the collapsed skin of a hand
whose flesh was changed within to empty space.
The sagging form shrouds the garden.
The arbor lies crushed under a wedding ring,
the yellow horn of a thumbnail seals the pond.

At the midpoint of each afternoon I wake
beside you, and study the clouds that cover us.
No detail there has altered. But the dead...
they seem almost to have moved since yesterday,
their cloudy bodies at a slow rolling boil.
Is it my fever that makes them shrink and swell?
And you, who never move—I would be with you.
But at the midpoint of each afternoon I wake.

III   MY METHOD

You have to wait for geese to be descending
a curving staircase of porous marble. It
will come down one day from swift glaciers
that glow in the sky, and coolness
will walk again in these burnt hills.

Then, swept from the board by the small
breathlike hand of blustery days,
nature and society lie upside down
in the puddles where they fell.
It's our youth come back: our youth
that once was simply our bodies' breath.
But now it sounds from far-off,
muffled in leaves, a hunting horn
that always follows deeper into the wood.

We hear it, grab torches and light out
to burn the ancestral home, with no concern
for where we will sleep tonight in the fatal weather,
tiles and lamps raining from the shaken dome.
For the right hand of fire rages out of control,
the left twists the doorknob of the body.

And we are more than ready to enter the bedchamber
where the angel of seventeen years
eternally grows more perfectly seventeen:
until she forgets the returning geese entirely,
dismisses her maids, and her looks are solely love.

But here we are always premature.
The fountain falls back exhausted,
and the delta of the vast waiting summer
conceals itself again, with the same
tenderness that marked its advent.
Perhaps with an angel my method is as useless
as sleep: restoring sleep, which women
in endless flocks returning at all seasons
rejoice to see in man between acts of love.

The Balloonist

Mother Mort humiliated me.
She said, "I'll be your only hope, your anchor,
your ballast and your balance. I'll keep
your bubble from the nausea of spinning
in its rushing off to everywhere."

Later that day, when we lifted from the shore
of an inland ocean of boiling antimony,
she lay in the bottom of the car
and not even the brightness of the air
was more transparent or more everywhere

than her nudity. At night when without wind
we slid out over the breathing starlit sea,
its white clutches returned beneath us to rushing foam.
There was starlight on the breathing of her hair
and it seemed that I was taking her somewhere.

As I Understood It

"As I understood it, living in the fountain,
the slow flower and fall of its angry rod
was destiny. And yet we had the power,
like a firework rocket that fails to burst,

to continue endlessly in imagination
for awaited stars. But water, in fact,
dropped back and ruffled the mirror of the source,
dispelling idle reflections, so that no man
could be tempted to drown himself for love.

"This is the sense then of your independence
in the surrounding garden of arms that rise and fall,
chopping meat. The silver thread
I wanted around your hips was more beautiful
than your current business: yourself
going before you,
dropping parts of your body by the road.
While you were at meat, my mouth was full of silver.

"I had ascended into heaven
vaguely, like water, only to be rudely dumped
on the plain way you snuffed the ground.
Now the peaches grow riper every day,
they ought to have fallen long ago,
and the too heavy brown spreads. I still want you
released from summer altogether,
like sunlight's color, which escapes the eyes."

This voice came back from a world of speculation
wrapped in the arms of a sister
to that lady whose ear it sought.
A peach tree frozen in the stark sunlit
half of its withered face, this globe drifts
in the black sea of star-encumbered night.

At the Hotel Oceano

They were such snobs that you and I alone
associated with the aging flowers.
The others laughed like a waterfall,
quarreled like the eternal dissatisfaction
of the warm breeze with everything,
and swallowed gaily all the stabbings
of tumescent keys with doors open
on a prospect of more of the same:
children practicing in the music room.

What were they but messengers
of the sun's growing old
too slowly for the eye to see?

Before the heartless-seeming
vengeance of it all, your beauty evokes
the poignant ice cube melting in a drink
abandoned before a Pacific sunset,
where distant pelicans,
symbols of mercy and succor, fish.

Immortal grapes hang in the leaves this fall,
fragments of sky, and we will drink them.
The promise is lost of saving everything
that passage turns to tears
as sparks forever in last summer's wave.
I may as well call you Chloe now,
my Beatrice. Your ancient beauty
is eaten by today for its satisfaction
to less than that bleached pelvis we see
afloat in the deserted sky.

THE EXCURSION

Through iron grills on storefronts, a low sun
twisted into my eyes from the black windows
where our car flashed in reflection, and I watched
our own reflections talking silently
beneath those surfaces: I saw you driving
while beside me your voice played with all
the interest of morning on the green edge of a cliff.

Five p.m. Out there crushed cups were spread
everywhere by feet. The opening doors were singing,
doors too full, spitting out the people,
who also yawned but with a hunger to swallow,
and you were telling your story: someone we knew
who had caught fire without apparent cause
and burned to death staring as usual at the walls.

My head rolled, appearing and disappearing
in the dry interrupted black glass river.

I looked at the women flowing past: long gauntlet
of pendulums, flashing scissors or, in the windows,
things displayed alive beneath crystal plates,
creatures in those waterways of a polished
darkness out of which the sun can't rise.

THE HYPNAGOGIC STATE

I

Again the dying spectrum.
Pacific salt.
The watery herd of new gods
thunders and falls between stone lips.
And the sounds of mating seep
rose and gold as through a Chinese screen.
Bodies of pure color mingle
under the night descending
from charcoal mountains,
vast wheat aswarm with flames.

And later in a steep alley over the sea,
in dead brick, which daylight always proves
riddled with lives, a slow hour strains for dawn.

Invincible sleep. The spectrum being born.
In the dog-eared court where light drops slowly
from leaf to leaf, a sundial,

water condensing on a twisted blade,

sweet outrage of the morning hour by sleep:

under an open window the lilac sleep,
in the dark cellar the wine of sleep,
whetted by first light the blade of sleep,
bees humming in the phlox of sleep.

Among tresses of moss
asleep at noon
a flower sucking the cracked numerical stone.

2

Rain falls to violet fingers
of girls, of beaten lilac
quivering where a gray wind
buries itself in sodden tassels.

An eye closes in damp cellars
under a forehead refreshed with saltless sweat.
Water
breaks from within,
from the yeast, from carcasses, eroded hills and blood,
springing purified when the image
of a dancer, fountain-shaped, relieves
the dripping earthen walls.

You are not here
but coolness mounts around her stained
feet and flows from her eyes. Her ankles
are garlanded in green feathers.

And red, a kiss
breaks ground in me, dagger
late in earth's summer.
Now I see us stand again on the highest turret,
our hair tangled in roots
trailing from a gray country that flees above.

All was sucked from us here below by hungry earth.
Only two vacuums are left, two painted shells
so light in the contorted air
we would need nothing, not even anklets of green wings,
to mount. It's time. Earth needs us
but to leap up, escape.
Northward over congealing seas
leading the ship heaped with dead
two forms glide, fused together,
their nipples coals, their groin the forge.

3

The lightning seeks and finds
a twisting way for its thread
through the solid blank of air:

water in riddled stone,
sequence of arches in deep walls.

And even if the storm were bells
ringing in one tower undersea,
softened and swaying in the currents,

or phosphorescence in a sealed cave,
a fetal tongue whose lips
long ago the surgeon closed,

it would come to you, not unasked.
The corpse of radiance
rises to the surface of ocean.
All the nights are thighs, glazed silk
stroked with a rod of amber.
And in the tiny laugh of static,
of light, a spark of purpose,
as the male repays a touch:

the fugitive
aurora in the flood.

4

In all your cities, queen and virgin,
is only the gelding,
huge muscle furbished with salt sweat,
burnt bays
dripping with the pure gods of earth,
and lodged in your body the vacuum cleaner,
a siren screaming for dirt.

Woman carved in warm topaz by this day,
you see a scepter gather its whiteness,
its flaring sky, swelling mountain.
Even now the power of cancer
awakes in you. In the temples
the quivering pillar squeezes blood
from its base of female heads.

Queen hugging your hollow waist
and looking seaward,
today a coffin made landfall,

a rotted trunk wrapped in vines.
A random wave threw it on the shore
with its skeleton,
a young man fleshless and memberless,
yet each bone
an immortal hardness.

And your sad tongue, your betrayer,
recalls how death in a dream didn't matter.
A kiss infused an endless pleasure.
You deny the climax

but the story forces your lips.

Reunion

Once we existed by violence but now
we are in gardens such as these.
The fear of entropy is banished to the kitchen,
the back chambers and passages
where our help gossips
and tastes the leavings of the party.

What could we do in our first blind rush
but take the arroyos constructed in the desert
by long-fled water
and cover their lips with moss?

In that city of neon lights and dust,
the wooden poles were the lobby's potted palms
in the Hotel des Baines, through which you slipped
to avoid me for another love you knew
was light and dust.

This is the sorrow that answers our questions here
among conversations and violins,
the shame of our old impossibility
that we hug, each alone, over which we laugh,
assured now that should everything withdraw
we still would spin through darkness,
two seeds in their husks.

La Belle Époque

Do you remember those nights in the Grand Hotel
when the sea had filled the harbor, had come
to wet the bluff's crest and spill
across the promenade, at last to lick
the top stair and the veranda's balustrade?

It was well known the water had halted there,
but everyone with less to lose than we
grasped the excuse of mortal fear and slept.
Abandoned by the servants, we soon found
there was no dinner, no music, nothing to say.

You were with me, weren't you, in that endless day?
I remember a man I'd never met who knew
your secret name. When I told him you were near,
he answered something I can't recall. That evening
we three sat staring carefully over the sea.

From our feet, crossing the water, the gray blade
of the darkening hotel's shadow slowly stretched
with dim suggestions of turret, arch and gable,
until at dusk it merged its mocking head
with the base of the silver dome's east wall.

Some who had been frightened by this shadow
insisted our drowning shadows lived in its rooms.
Others thought it a bridge or road, though none
risked a try at escape. And you said nothing:
unduped, as I suppose, by dreams of description.

Why do I tell you, when you know what it was
and understand it well? But I see again
black marble corridors hiding small flames at night
in polished floors, flowing through open doors
to level aisles of stars on the hard sea.

After nightfall, no one would stir for fear
that the enthralled eyes accepted as gleaming parquet
a surface which to the body was dark sea.
We sat in wicker chairs and let those nights
efface their memories, each of the one before.

So I know little of that time, though maybe all.
For what was there except by intellect alone
to maintain the motions of the bored heart and lungs?
Do you remember how no one could explain
why it was that we wanted to never die?

WHAT BECAME OF THE SHEPHERD

At first there's the little golden cage
with blue ceiling. Shreds fall from it like hairs
and lie curled
as shadows on the plain. At twilight
a puny wail emerges, reminding someone
of a bee caught long ago in a glass jar.
Nervous it grows and angrier
as the sound of an airplane going somewhere
approaches and fades, and even the wind,
that servant of a slave's fevers and chills,
sings of perpetually leaving. But here
the mad humming is and here it stays,
though certain intimations of now silent birds
made the fact invisible this morning.

All at once in his wicker chair appears
the old one. And in the blustery season
once a week the sullen forecast
of his voice breaks through the cloudy lips
in concert with some meager escape of sun:

"O brighter islands in the sleety spring,
look forward to a thermonuclear crocus
soon to break ground and compose
its eclogue: *The Rout and the Rut of the Iceman.*
I the destined remnant am prepared
for my lone cave, my gleeful thoughts:
how the pot iron alembic burst
in the mortal disease of its cooking.
I told them. And my death
will be unique, the death of the last man.
I will be singular, leave cleanness after me,
be free, have nothing to do
with the maps where X always turned out to mark
the spot, the ruins of the place
we had started from that morning."

—Come into the garden, darling. Here's Father,
much changed from the man you remember.
Say "Hello," Father. He knows us, he just refuses
to admit it. His illness seems almost willful,
it has such fervor, though who can say
what he has to be mad about: we're none of us
getting any younger. He won't eat
and yet he doesn't want to die, he wants
revenge and to live forever. The tighter
those gray gums shut, I think, the harder
he's sucking on some bitter orange.

IV   Whose Invention Was This

Far-off your small hand lies this evening
across the prairies.
The curvature of earth objects like sleep
to the cohabitation of our eyes.

Whose invention was this nasal ballad rising
toward the glances of arc-light stars?
Among the frayed beach umbrellas
of a Breton fall, this cigar meditating?
This manuscript angel in the innocence
of his battered trunk, who sees the moon
descend each midnight, an ice cube,
into his already lukewarm toddy?

From all this the last trump of your mouth
and the mute of your present vis-à-vis, the sausage,
are safe behind more than the girth of Indiana.
The waffle iron of Nebraska.
Ohio's radium oven. Alarm clock
of northern Illinois. Wisconsin word game,
electric blanket of Iowa turned up to ten,
satisfied Minnesota off to work.
Even astral California
locks up the desk at night, even Germany
hides something amusing under its stylish tweeds.

Behind the transparent Chinese screen of air
in the ballroom corner, even the dental student
has his long pivotal tooth, even the store owner
his barely visible mainmast.

Hypnotic sundial, you have the night and your herd
of watery boys and a home movie camera
and the turned back of the fat chaperon, earth.

CUT FLOWER

To varnish its topless lilium
with jealousy, your burning bush
overcame him. It was loud,
calling across a bed of white meat, unslept-in,
mixed with the wind, voice of hallways.
First the hero's backward glance had fallen
on his youth of mother-of-pearl linoleum
depressed over cold bulbs planted in the floor.
He had known love: plumes of blue fire the breeze
bent eastward when they would fountain
from shallow wells under the golf greens.
Such space had filled those days:
thousands of faintly colored images
cast in glass tinkled
between the observer and everything, until
your headless ardor descended on its occult
object like the nostalgia of colonialists:
a punch in the face. The apparent result
seeped as if blood into the skin,
a bruise or a blush: the lily
starts in contemplation of its anger:
nothing resembles more the first shoots
rising from a mold of disease.
And now he is proof against the mild entrancing
memorious chill of the spring weather.
He's bound elsewhere, entirely run wild
and unnatural. A decision has been made
in his deepest hair, setting him free
or, as they say, uprooting him.
He empties faintly whispering
gelatinous green water from his earthen vase.
There is heard the jewel-faceted lyric
of distant tides moving in shadow
while the earth's black skirts remain
lowered as yet: a reticence that is
the playfulness of a woman great example
has shown the thing she wants

and to wait for him with purpose, like a gardener,
till death. The bulb is in caverns
of her expecting, in the colorless dark,
red and swollen as meat filling with blood.

The Future of Two Illusions

The plugs and sockets were perfectly mated
and the juice began to flow. From the flying machine
we looked down through a cloud crevice,
fascinated, at this obscene ceremony.

For suddenly we saw the exciting chance
of a tunnel beneath the Alps,
which even if you were Italy and I were France
might bring me to you. But did we need it?
We had a gyroplane, we had a zeppelin,
a bird harness, a mechanical maple seed.

The scene drew its power of illusion
from the rhythm of subterranean machinery,
lub-dub lub-dub, and a sudden recognition:
trolls were pumping ichor up to our sky
through lacework veins we dodged among,
a bee in the trellis with ivy and rose entwined.

Just then I heard your parachute
puff open behind: now you were only a cloud
weeping back to the earth. Today
not even your gift of solitude consoles me
for the way you dropped, an egg, into the sweet
suicide cake of already sickly spouses.

Song

We two would have gone together
like bread and butter;
fat in my bloodstream, you growing old alone;
an eggshell and turning into a road map;
mild light in September and a vacuum cleaner.
Like a little boy and a muddy cellar,
solitary vice and a mirror,

a head of hair and a razor.
Like a tongue and a pair of scissors.
Like hope and an accurate forecast.

Though all you wanted, as you used to say,
was "sitting before the fire
before you, dear, like a naked girl
just under the surface of the water.
Sewing, like a film version of the unabridged *Arabian Nights*.
Children in our middle years
like passenger dolphins
docking in the fountain of youth.
In fact, television like Ayesha's fire.
I am not without imagination.
I am used to looking far away
at the impossible penises
of my desire. It creates, indeed,
this furry mirror of my gaze,
which was for a while your ornamental codpiece.
It added a lot to my way of thinking.
But since then I've had to stop
at your place, see
under the open window the lilac of sleep,
in the dark cellar the wine of sleep,
around the raised cradle the maple canopy of sleep,
beside the door the rhododendron of sleep,
and bees humming in the phlox of sleep."

MOTIVE OF THE JOURNEY

"My dear, the flabbergasted flags dithering on your poles
will deliver me to where I came from.
For example, the organizer of your cake,
who upholds the moist chewiness of your members
as compensation for the lack of air.
The light expectorated from your eyes
the way a hungry helmet lamp drools on a coal seam.
A replica of the Bridge of Sighs possesses my ear and retails
the smirk and loosened thighs of quite a sunset,
and the fact that suddenly I am only this one ear
turns the water of my loins
with its sappy need to be drunk
to toothpaste.

If I am to be a single ear,
I'd rather be lying in Gethsemane
with the memory of a recent stinging rebuke,
listening to the rose appear through the ice of the sky.
My childhood and my own country come to mind,
the violin singing behind the wet tower,
but here its ghost will only play 'Liebestraum'
and only the tears of things erupt from
the phallic features of the landscape
to descend into the odd black space in front of you.
Contemplating it, the whirlwind of longing reaps me.
I sweat this blood because my next appointment
is with the agony of the threshing floor,
to be screened for my passport."

Ruefully the bearded comet who had been speaking
discarded the insurance tables forecasting death at seventeen
and set sail for outermost Flora, root of his tongue.
There these same poles grow but as trees.
Social flags hold perpetual symposium overhead
and spread a cool table on the ground.
Waiting for lunch, he's drinking in the shade
and he remembers leaving you as the frenzy
of crushing grapes. This wine remains a song forever
in the throat's joy and the sculpture of the glass.

THE BIRDS STAY FAR AWAY

To you my words are important as a spoon
thrust in the fol-de-rol of night
and the fixed stars to drop it as usual

into your tearlike eyes ashiver
and down the hairless slopes far underneath,
which will to sag since the nature of things

has said so. Yet that is only part of it.
Something still smaller than the diminishing fate
of our kiss at the bottom of the stairs

is swimming in your drowned certainty
about what we were born. Do you
appease it, O my parasol, you cried to me

as you became a cloud that sheltered you
from you the huge blue girl
abandoned and raining down her look of light

as tears. I say permit me understand you,
permit me egress from this your hopeless love
through your hopeless hate into you.

You are everything that can be seen from here,
as in yuletide an impression of perpetual overcast
maligns the brilliant light of winter.

So you insist that we leave hand in hand
into the sunset that can't escape us,
evening permanent now, literally nothing

making sense anymore
escape from the fonts and altogether
talk in transparent rose.

Thus I was married to you underground
with an original purpose
of following and going on beside you

into a house of prayer that was to have been
the landmark pointed far forward
at our wedding night of endless acceleration,

a village cherishing the blood
back into its slaughtered lamb. Then we
emerged in quiet snow and ice,

in the no excitement
of growing less, the bad faith
of again next year. But we could leave it

to those corpses to be those tears.
What if something weighty ballasted you
descending the staircase,

a silence as embarrassing as small talk?
From this except us, lest the birds
stay far away, nothing known,

the birds who beyond their farthest feathers
in pure flight are you.
Forget it. Resign yourself and recall:

this day was destined to be light
as your conception in the old days,
ten nonexistent cities where you want to go.

LOVED ONES

The division they had made was too simple:
love and hate, like lunacy and madness.
In truth their work is a blindness
of many rooms, each a spacious ignorance
crystalline and pure as to a bee its bottle.

Nor did their legionaries whom we slew
vengefully in the caves—claw-footed tables,
the limp carnivorous glove, those mouths
called keyboards—fall around any shadow that cast up
from itself the solidity of a man.

So there we were, arraigned in the nurseries,
the parlors, music rooms and bedrooms,
listening to them adjust to their new life
as a burst balloon that demands emulation.

And at each close of day the child fills up
with hunger, hearing the lost shouts of other
children invisible beneath marshaled trees
outside his high dark window. Clothed in leaves,
the lesseners of night open yellow eyes
to watch him envision the last chance:

Lovers' Leap, where he and the faceless partner
fall eagerly into dreams of falling. In the fields
gently she lays down as it is the law
and erects him as a fountain.

Believe It or Not, You Love Me

When the wings arrive
to suck from the crystals of salt and sugar
their heartbeat feathers, you'll see again
the tall fountain-haired man you dreamed:
the one who went into a little basement café
but the stairs took him to the center of the earth.
His movement down was the falling of a bomb
and our disembarkation, known as morning,
was the quick gesture you used to throw away
your hat with the plumes of fly-ash and sulphur vapor.

The action has revealed our eyes in time:
we glimpse slimed buttocks, spleens
built of black glass, and the twisted I-beam
of someone's spine fall gratefully
into a hot bath beyond mountains
beyond which there is obviously nothing.
It would be enough, I thought, to lie awake here
guarded by a palisade of wheat
while the people living on the sky
provided dreams.

                Interesting people
on their cupped soil into which the dust
falls, where water meets and marries it,
where the carefully developed thought of rain
at first boils formlessly and then as stalks
bursts upward toward us here,
delivering on its topmost leaves
some flavor of that country we only know
from the vantage of its destiny.

                        But you
are not content. You've found in a clearing
in a gray-blue forest rigged with webs
a vast checkerboard. The polished black
squares are the days sealed over
with glass to let us look but not plunge in
from despair or thirst. And the red squares of blood,
are they the sea in which are islands, or lakes
in a dark land?

              Here you lie down
and the mooring threads of the stars
ray to your navel. Here
you want me to save you by speaking clearly
of white unintelligible things. You lie
alone in your yellow windswept bed
and my part is to appear speaking on the lintel
with the anger of a fountain poised for flight.

ONE LAYS HIS HAND ACROSS FISSURES

All the aquamarine inlay of the hand-tooled
phoenix-hide binding of devotion:
troglodytic huge Latin and more Greek
today. Today irresistible sleep
blows a kiss to the dog collar. Is it
the seed, however, of that old knight sans blowtorch
armored in the stiff love of you?

We have our interlocking tongues and
the secret of the vacuum seal,
much like the paternity suit of midnight,
who wants a name for some spaces.
But are the spaces truly spaces, as between
notes on a piano?—one lays his hand across fissures
and a music scrambles to safety.

And now it's everywhere, filling the distances
between the lightbulb, the mirror and the bed,
we tesserae at last in our baptism of glue.
I felt the world beginning to go right
when a Siamese lesbian (or two?) hired me
for a human dildo. Their house now, it can't
be helped, is in opposition, bursting with sons.

V   SHADE

Before you were born, beauty's summer died.
Now at times it brushes you
with its abstract wing, like a virtue,
something from a world where bodies have no bodies,
are as real as names and produce no tears.

Here the sounds of the beautiful ideas,
heard or unheard, sit looking down through mist
at leaves that are browning or will brown,
and on both sides of the window the water
slowly condenses and rolls earthward.

So a thought of time dwelling in a timeless place
will fall, if a tree dares to dash across the sun.
A blow of shadow strikes your sleep in whitened light.
But has your day come too soon, stayed too long,
that the skin is dry now, an expectation of flame?

Again the image: days passing beneath oaks
to nothing but further days, further knowledge
of the sky held in fingered leaves:
it empties you into confusion.
Metamorphosis is pain and in pain
you look now through the eyes of some animal.
Of all that is visible, nothing remains
marked out as yours in the soft, darkened afternoon.
Far away the tree-aisles dim
to nights that, entered, are not nights
but other limbs of this day
held in stroking shadow.

And that ancient being, you, sole citizen
of the shadow, waits, echoing with muted light;

alone, cannot pronounce itself alone,

expecting someone, expecting pleasure:

nor shall you brag it wanders in death's shade.

A Leaf

"There are so many diseases. How
can a man avoid them all?" he said,
his eyes gliding, charioted upon
the golden leaves. A golden leaf
tottered to rest on his shoulder
and became one tattered wing.

Yes, in the form of this leaf the ghost
of the buried and forgotten
organs of flight returned and spoke:
"There is only one disease.
You have been loving it all summer."

RECUPERATION

If there is such a thing as love,
I saw it in your letter, which they gave me
when I was out of danger. "Your heart
(you wrote) is as obscene a thing
as I ever hope to meet. And when I saw
how it was trying to explode on me
in a deluge of germinal phlegm
and how you crawled all over it,
begging it to hold back...well, frankly,
I was revolted. So in the future
you and your terror just keep away from here.
In repugnance, Your Everything."

Now I admit I'm dying
and I don't worry anymore. Not about
dissolving into a flood of intercourse,
not about anything, unless it is
that the nearness of your quiet face, my sister,
should speedily raise me from my bed.

WOODGATE

The oak tree's bole is open: I go in
and lift the trap that opens on the roots.
A web falls over my hair as I climb down.

The interior of a granite egg
is the sky here, an even purple light
shifts across a meadow of yellow grasses.
I lie on my face and young trees
start to define me, growing around the borders
an ambitious illusionist cut long ago
into the slug, my body.

Once this center was a spinning,
a sucking hole, an indrawn breath, a desire.
I'm still as if you have no use for me.
I remember your face now: it grew,
a knot, a sign in the fissured bark.

I remember, moored to the trunk, a boat
beating on the silver edge of a sea.

Morning Fragments

The ledger vanishes in the flood again.
The blue bowl pours, warm liquid fills this air,
melting the block of ice that held you.
Now vast blindness is a legend that eddies away
into crumbling warehouses,
the hearts of evergreens,
your throat.

What survives there is the wish to recall
the clear plan of your days
and of all to come. And the morning fragments,
growing visible, seem to rebuild themselves
out of twilight, mildew and melancholy
toward an edifice still darkened in you:
as if this new hour were not yet morning
but the ghost and messenger of morning.

And were you here yesterday already?
Did your feet, as now, mark out a track
through the glassy moisture of the lawn,
and even then were you following
faint prints of a day before? Today
you determine to remember everything.
You will know at last if the sun ages
or is created every dawn
out of nothing at the surface of the sea.
You will know if this dayspring is eternal
or lies on a heap of others,
a page just turned, reversing all.

And meanwhile night has sunk as a hedge
sinks into distance as you walk away.

Voices were making explanation behind it,
something you might have understood, some secret
of a former life. But glowing spaces outward,
poplar spires and domes of the willows,
were newly before you then, they drew you on,
so that now you will never know what was being said,
if something is lost forever,
or if much, happily,
is put behind you and forgotten.

Food for Three Days

Dumpling soup and sardines on crackers.
Sardines and salami on crackers.
The sun impassive in the wet tar.

Sardines and salami on crackers.
A little sugar in the canned beans.
The sunset impulsive in the streaked window.

A little sugar in the canned beans,
a dozen peaches in a polished window,
like the sunset of morning

a dozen peaches in a polished window.

Eyes Pared to the Gleam

You were saying, "Dreams
are in the confection of verbs:
something dead and almost weightless,
maybe a puppet's arm,
is caught in the web a spider hung,
and then under her slight stress
it makes us a sign."

To the east someone was pulling out a sword
of hard lights, like eyes pared to the gleam:
Orion, his arms stiff, the night
draped over him, a bat-wing cloak,
and at least thirty years before our sun
diving up from the sea.

Moon

The succulence and insouciance of the moon.
Red dust falling from the brickyard moon.
The companionable presence of the railroad moon
and the factory moon's silver whistle.
I've heard the moon croaking to the big frogs,
the creek moon, hiding down in the cattails.
If only the moon would shut up,
the lover's moon, laughing all alone
like closing the gate behind your solitude on a moonless night.
Who believes anymore in the sympathy of the moon
despite the grayness of the moon's face,
the way the moon gets fat,
the horrible lingering explosion of the moon,
the white hair of the moon falling on the earth,
the new hyacinth moon,
the moon fluttering like a sparrow that has made it through winter,
the pitiful jobless remnant of the moon,
the boredom, the endless pregnancies, the childlessness of the moon?
The moon was laughing as I closed the gate.
A flashlight in the woods, the moon
glinted, a glazed eye open in the moonlight,
moonlight shining on a white rock
whose moss has withered under the glance of the moon.
I thought of the trash barrel moon,
banana peels illuminated by the moon,
the black expectant gape of the silent moon
like a toilet bowl the moon lights through a window.
I spread my arms—as if stabbed by you, O moon,
and lifted up, a fish on the arrow of the moon.
Then in the day, the white moon shrank
like a woman behind a gate. Moon, the dead women
are piling up like dried moon husks.
I shout only to women, moon,
and in the silence of the moon's circular riot
they have turned to sand. My moon shadow
is the hardest thing to forget but the vapid moon.
My small sex would annihilate this moon.
What a man generates can the moon bear?
There is no space in our nights for this moon.
At sunrise the moon kissed a woman on her plumed crest.
She was lifted toward the moon's now empty station.
A pillar of water, I raised the coal of that new moon.

Anniversary in a Private Room

Despite the mystical design of a lost religion
that seals the wall where a window ought to open,
it seems to us now that time goes past
more slowly outside, in expectation
of stopping in the garden for which we plan.
It seems that, by the river, a man says to his wife,
"The blueprint I gave you
was a tracing of your mother's skeleton.
In those days of our sad youth proclaiming
war between knowledge and desire,
we had never been anywhere but all over the world.
And we wrote those laws that night."

We nod our heads. They might have known
that part of us is night,
how it turns over in its grave and is recalled
by this accident to morning.
Everything gets one last chance,
just as tomorrow will. And though your foot
slips now and then with a faint cry in the tremor
of an earth built slowly of disappointed fathers,
still you press a seedhole and drop in
a motive for the words to come,
as immense as allegorical temples
in the landscape of the body.
And in earliest spring, already, the tiny ear-flowers
hear the verse of bees arrowing from future time
to wet their feet in this excited dust
and spread it everywhere, and smear it
all over the bleached pelvises of cities.

Meanwhile, nothing disturbs your joy, O queen
of this endlessly inventive melody,
human aria for which
the circular left hand of the orchestra
has long waited, perfecting itself
in the grievous beauty of its flaws.
Nothing, except that now and then your voice
breaks when you are suddenly laid asleep
by the sight of a dead man on a bone-white street
laughing with friends as he enters an office door:
for no one ever appears far-off

on our horizon here, approaching our gate
through the telescopic clarity of this air.
How lonely you sometimes seem
in the infinity of your unknown hope,
walled up in silent prayer. And the insolent,
unyielding hieroglyph closes the lips
around the promise of being as you are.

Saying Here

The owls, though hung to death in tangled air
and twirling idly, interposed a grace
between our heads and a jealous moon.
In a field pitted with smallpox
you had planted this gladiolus dawn.

Now high in the trees of a new forest
fungi remold the carcass of a ship
set there gently by waves that crushed the port.
Asleep on the bow and angry in the stern,
with squirrels as lookouts, we drift.
For the anchor was eaten by this sea
to rust: an exhilaration in the air,
a trace of the earth's blood.

In this channel that always flows both ways,
a retrospect gives us the end of life:
swashbuckling devotion among abortions,
and beneath a surface of flies
the goal of the bathysphere of morning incoherence:
in the park between a ruined tower
and a temple still imageless, the swallows
are darting through a fountain,
it's evening, and we three set out for town.

BLACK ORCHID

Ulysses en Route

Rock. Sun and rock.
And all day long naked feet
falling on the rock and the sun
falling like a drop of lead into the brain.

So I retain the image of the meager world
that now amid crowded flotsam
in shipwreck, in absence, I desire:
not as relief but as
the true adventure, dusty
spring, spaces where the cypress
denies denial, hurling waves
upward of blue-green foamed to gold.

It is to be unborn
in branching tunnels,
this custody of the wind's treasure
that must not be touched, this knowledge
of swine born of the intercourse
between men and the sun's power, this wisdom
from the powerless dead. But am I lifted
back toward that first sun mark
on these upheavals of the torn bursting crest,
in the circular storm that rolls
in night's groundless sphere?

And still, I am an idea,
this is a breath of envy
to men who hear of these adventures
and have not looked in their own house.
Banal to me as glances in a mirror,
as strengths unacknowledged, are these courses
in the world's belly,
regions like bowels serving the lighted flesh,
these palaces
and courtesies hidden in the supporting
ocean, huge parodies of man,
equations of harmony and sleep.

I'd return to that blazing
where slime is turned to brick. O for sleep
to pour again

from walls catching fire at noon,
for summers stretching like a knotted rope,
for my arm bent to all the broken
stones that wasted me, strong illusion
of boredom, spur of this plunge
into the lungs of this blue breast's swelling.

And not at all can the jealousy
that is yours, who watch, left behind
on stretching beaches, redeem for me
the journey. Now I know
how to breathe the golden dust
of my threshing floor and not be turned to gold.
In the fields, thrown by the sun
more invincible each day, I could laugh
like a young wrestler now
foreknowing an end to his weakness.

From Mean Families

We awoke in mean families,
the air filled with seeds.
In our rooms a huge confusion
of soldiers
and markets dissolved into loud shouts
that penetrated every wall.
Even the wafer of bread you gave me
and the wafer of metal I returned
were seized between us by aerials
and transmuted to a voice
that sold bandages to our wrists.
Now the bars of the cell move with us,
they seem to be the fingered shadow
of that orange hand over the sun,
the shadows of the bald trees.
We have been forgotten here
in this mansion, this vast estate
where the streams are wrung
from the bodies of those who have lost us.
In the pudding that appears, the game
materializing at our least desire
on the glass table,
we recognize their blood, their limbs.

The only season here is autumn.
And in the late afternoon, when mist
obscures the far shore of the ornamental lake
and creates a sea, we stand
where the clear stream silently enters.
Let the missionary come back
from the interior.
Let him repeat the acts of his faith,
which struggles now and vanishes in us
with the torpor of the clouds.

Poem

The unheralded mystery of spring
forces its will again on the herald flower.
In the thicket I pause to remember.
February was my mentor in misery,
that hollow pamphlet from yellow skies,
basin of dead sparrows.
I am a glove on an absent hand
and speaking, writing are nothing but the dream.
Don't try to say they are anything more than dream.
Whether or not there is such a thing as time,
I am this window on night's senseless palette,
which is already the portrait
more perfect than the face.
Across the torn darkness
I am this anarchic scrawl,
this wake of a restless scalpel.

Gone South

The gray hair turning gold,
the white eyes turning
blue followed us
as we rode the snake's back
twisted among columns of water.

We burst
like wild canaries
from a collapsing twig,

and floated to this white basin,
this pool the mirror of flashing sand.
Here water is a dust so fine
its particles, grown less than nothing,
have sifted through being's wall and live
on the other side. But swimming
in them, here we remain: the sun points out
doors flashing everywhere in the water,
never open where we are. The days float
surrounded by red sirens here,
silent alarms of blood,
songs of the perfect weather.

Look at the bougainvillea
spilling from your wounds.

Night, and a man made of water
stands just outside the window near your bed,
leaning on the faint sill, whispering.

Beneath homecoming pelicans
the fish put themselves in our hands
and rain closes its silver teeth around us
as a veil. We are playing hearts
under a tree of fans.

On the stairs, later, and in the halls,
you meet all the forms of desire,
some naked but for sandals of a blinding glare,
some wrapped in cloaks, who secretly
stare after you
from fern beds
under cupped palms.

We watch the salesman sold as slave
to a queen
whom once he kidnaped from her father,
raped and threw away.
Now he is happy at last,
yoked in the days,
beaten at dusk,
with her moist ribbon.

In the stone streets, our thought
scraped from the walls each moment
by a white knife,
we are happy for this tin table in the shade
with its plastic flower,
sign of an enduring spring.

Flashes of heat pass by.
You are drinking
the bottle of orange pop you ordered
and it's the sun, the sun,
cool, liquid, and sweet,
sustaining our life
even
in the center of its light.

The Naturalist

When my heart first began to stutter
so no one could understand it
(they guessed it was prophesying death),
then I had second thoughts. I moved
here to this slope in a line of mountains
facing another line of mountains
like men facing women at a dance.
Eighty-eight years in the city. I recall
a phrase: "up and down" or was it "back and forth?"
And something about tires, revolving and revolution,
and the gratefulness of sleep, the fact that
everyone I knew was slipping away,
building up a mask of wood. So little
remains of that, like the sweat of breath on a window
shrinking to give the view again.
Now I plan to sit here and watch the weather
roll down this aisle to the valley,
as today. Everything is reversed
from what it was. Lighted paths of rain
wind as though upward from the overcast
into a ragged green sky: the trees.
Unmoored islands, the clouds
pass in a rhythm,
blue spaces between. A sun comes out
from their trailing edges: a kind of morning

climbing from horizons overhead
toward a zenith in the earth. Today
there were seven mornings in the storm.
I plan to sit here: maybe the chances
will give two years to compare with one another.
I've heard of "new growth," the intangible
difference of one spring from the last,
which evades memory, too small,
too simple for the mind.
I wonder what I will make of it?
One ring closer to all I want?

Black Orchid

A black orchid convokes bees
at your body's center,
a stem of urine
connects it to the ground.
Near where you stand, the fishes
leap up an arc of light
and hang in a rainbow
over the disgorging cleft.

We are sad while we live here.
We hate this summer for the fleshy children
who force themselves as food into our eyes
closed toward the future.
Then the summer swells,
it will not last forever.
How we long for deliverance
as the lizards show and disappear
between the white rock
and the leaves: blue and green,
little replicas of how the sky's
acid meets and etches
the temple of the palm forest.

And looking into the region
of that burning, with what desire
earth is moved
continually to pour itself.
The fountain raises its head

and with water's passionate vengeance
loses all
to color the dry rock with these flowers.

LEVELS

This day of smoke and grating, of women
screeching like harried gulls, preserves us
from the fantasy that anything contains
all that we lack. On this beach by a slate-gray
ocean roofed with slate-gray sky,
the weeds are durable and last
several years, while imperceptibly
their replacements creep in among them.
The crabs hiding in tidal sand to breed
aspire to the tortoise's endurance, and the rocks
are stronger, or the bright grains
of pure silicon imitating an absent sun.
Someday the last of all these present
will wear away, be recombined,
and all will have started anew
or anew insofar as it concerns us,
though a little older; as in bodies
the cells succeed each other and the face
is almost the same, yet stiffened. So
we think to try the winding stair we found
cut in the stone of the sea cliff: maybe it leads
to a city or village on a plain above,
at least to an encampment of goatherds, some people
noble enough to have once had fathers
with power to imagine and to carve these steps.
Or would we find only another beach,
the clouds we see above us now
becoming there the roaring surf
that reaches for the ankles, drowning thought,
with above it another sky muffling in mist
another bluff? Even so, our life would be
changed from what we know, though no one
could describe the difference or recall
our former homes; it would be a progress
like that from yesterday to today.
There as here the smoke of our fires
would thicken the morning fog, there too

the shouting gulls would glide stonelike
in and out of sight through the gray
mist that condenses in their eyes.

NORTHERN SPRING

I

The spring
we longed for,
invoked from our bed,
hid itself.

Out of the black eve
of Easter
only snow.

And at dawn we went
to find how deeply
earth was buried again.

Winding out
into the gray, rocky haze
of beaten trees,
the only mark:
track of a lone hare,
which we followed
for want of another sign.

Through the maze of barren stems
under the plucked crown
we followed
to a treeless opening, a glade
where the tracks left their line
to weave and dance among
brown branches of the scrub
lifted above the snow.

Naked on the snow
the branches flourished
deep in a light
that opened suddenly overhead,
a world and flesh extended
from the star to the bone:

another life, a life that we
had hoped not to find,
sprung from the failure
of our season to be born.

2

The light brims
just under the surface of your flesh.

Sometimes
a blow touches you and the light shrinks, recedes,
you darken.

And the light comes back,
slowly,
through blue, through orange:
colors of the bruise.

Comes back
to itself, to you,
form of the sun

casting your halo
here in the shadow of the wing.

3

The frogs sing
to the bones of the reeds
to put on flesh.

A blackbird, a waiting heart,
stirs
in the defrauded ribs.

4

This April again
in the mud
the poor are waiting for the leaves.

Again in the summer that comes
we will see the garden
from far-off,

from the paths and temples,

our vision
mediated by the air
of music, of conversation.

The poor, whose only clothing
is summer, will feel
on their still grateful sides
how the larvae
puncture the fabric,
how October tears the sleeves,
will see it happen,

perpetually awake
in the rain
in the night
under the deserted bridge
in a rag of the seasons.

5

Of growing crevices,
this troubled day.
Cracked earth, cracked sky.
Uninhabited
light and darkness
flow out, mingling
in one emptiness
under the trees.

The dominating presence
is the absent.
Light falls into
spaces
waiting, yesterday
deserted quietly.

This inconsolable day,
parted
from its members,
an immobile stirring
between the moist and the dry,
drags itself:

body of the real,
stump of the dream.

6

Today, this crippled day,
this strange day,
is growing thin.
The light is sinking
from the surface of its flesh.

Shivering, it steps into me.

Lie there
with your words, your gestures
fading and their ghosts fading.

You too will rise
when the grave opens.
A new light
will treasure the grace
of your least motion.

THE PAUSES

As children we would search
the ground for signs,
certain a language had been planted there
by purpose, its recovery to lead
to a destination, some knowledge
deposited for us in a hidden place.
We read broken twigs in the woods,
spots of paint on the grass,
or blood. Openings among the stems
of dense bushes along the creek
to us were a trail, now useless,
where someone had passed long ago.
We followed arrows, numbers,
crude signs painted on sidewalks
across the city: they turned
and re-entered themselves, circles
the adults told us later
were marks of men planning sewers.

And we came to unexpected things:
a tunnel of woven brush
floored with soft mulch that led
to a round hall of higher bushes
filled with green light; a shelf
of the creek bank thrust out under
a veil of vines from the trees,
where we saw the bass
pierce a reflection of the sun
among reeds. There the huge willow
was a faceless virgin weeping
over the stream while we stood
in the pit of her eyes and lips.
Or if one of us went out alone
in the earliest light, often
he would find a place of total still
though not silence: the fly
and goldfinch spoke from far-off
to his isolation in tall grass
under a clear bell
of sunlight turning to light
all impressions of all bodies.
A strange idleness always met
the adventurer led by chance traces
(the only fruits of our careful science)
to ends of calm looking, hearing, feeling,
of warmth passing into the body
at the base of the neck, of long moments
melded to a scent of weeds
in the memory. And was this in fact
all we wanted the signs to point at?—
this peace as common as air
yet entered only when a pause
that seemed endless
fell, strengthening the curious one
to abandon it again.

On the Song of the Men

We would sing in the fields:
green billows fermenting around us,
through which we walked, we fought.
And each note became a small animal
that ascended through light wind

as if running up a stair. Behind us,
you were in bed, wrapped in your white
cloak of linen, the invisible cloak
that rises each morning to stand beside you,
later moving off and dissolving
in the doorway. We moved
ever farther from one another,
each one down the twisting aisle
made by his sickle in the corn
taller than a man. Only our song
still held us together, growing fainter,
till I seemed to hear the others
only as I heard you: the treasured rustling,
the bright aurora when you slightly turn
in your open vault, far away.
On the horizon, concealed from our eyes
by the stalks, there was water
and above it a fine haze
gathering into form:
a white wing, a moving sail.

THE RAVINE

To this shelf of rock so many movements
carry the things that wear the names.
Messengers, no things in themselves:
the different kinds of distance—to rocks,
to the ailanthus clump;
the kinds of heat that rise from the glowing
banks, warping the slope of weeds,
and are changed to coolness among
bearded syllables of a word
that day by day flows over.
The wind gives sudden bows
to each spire of grass,
to each its own style of address:
gifts of the air
pouring into the hollow
and down on the green spaces of river
shining in the gaps.
The purple thistles bob,
poplars choosing not to decide
sway and snatch their leaves
continually from silver into green.

A hushed noise rests all around,
choired in the glowing distances,
one locust and one bird
melding nameless music, the sounds
married in scent that also
has no name: a scent
shaken by the wind, lifted by noon
to this shelf of rock.
Here the first man returns
to his nude and mute survey,
to the voids of his speech
in which he perishes, worn out
by ghosts who offer themselves
and always unanswered escape.

SECOND PERSON

To think of you is to dream.
You stand in the arch free of any wall
at the top of the crumbling stair
cut in the cliff side. Beyond you
the field returns heat to the sky
transformed into musk, men of foam
leaning on their elbows float
in the perfumed water, a go-between
light continually promotes desire,
and none of them is as naked as you are.

To look closely at you reveals
nothing but blood floating in milk,
the reminiscence of repeated disaster
delicately nursed. But this
is hard to remember, for your essential color
is the pale gold fountain
that leaps between your fingers and your look.

"In the morning," you seem to say,
"you will find me in the woods,
asleep at the base of an oak tree.
At first you will catch a single gleam
and think it's a fallen sapling stripped of bark."
But when we reach you, there's only a door
open at the verge of empty air.

The Wasp

At noon
sleeping beside a pine tree
I was awakened by a huge cross
laboring through the air
roaring loudly
its head turned toward the ocean.
With what misery
what fortitude what drowsiness
a wasp on that last warm day of October
picked its way
in the castle of magnetic needles
bristling toward a million points
each indicating snow.
But at last it fell to the earth.
"When" it asked me
"will you quit waking up
scaring away the star of June
from your forehead
the clear vista
high paths among mountains of water?"
And indeed armies of ghosts
were fleeing
across the shaking grass
were tearing the woods apart
in their panic
spilling into the river.

These Dwarves

In the mornings I like things very clear
and these dwarves oblige me
like a firm stone island in a mudslide.
Among the paratroopers dropped by science
from above the clouds
they are happy exhibiting their smoky stammers
that fog the edges of the well-honed leaves.
They are slower than a track
abandoned by all trains,
so slow that by merely being the whole world
blurs and burns itself in the friction of rushing past them.
For the traveler who catches sight of them,

they assume the expression of crows who have swallowed diamonds.
And from their bowels the diamonds pronounce
the moves of a chess game
and in the diamond language moan popular songs
that emerge in the crow language
as directions to a lost mine.
At dawn, however, these dwarves reveal themselves
as signposts the wind and rain have erased.
On their hunched backs they bear a spectrum
from coagulated purple to the sparsest orange,
and though sometimes they appear to move,
if anyone grasps their shoulders he touches wood.

THE QUEST OF THE EGG

Who first posed the quest of the egg?
Not only the adventure's author
but also its point and its reward:
these things are lost in antiquity.
And meanwhile in this room
there's not enough room to turn around
and I can't imagine where an egg might be hidden,
can you? When I first came aboard,
I asked the captain about our destination.
"Who can say what is destined?" he replies.
"As for me, I make hats. We encounter
various rainbows and a different hat
is appropriate to each rainbow." It's common here,
this exact calculating of one's social duties
as a leaf calculates its fall. The opinion
of the engineer on the point of destination
is that it doesn't matter since the rules
preclude leaving this stateroom: outside
there might be eggs as common as diamonds
on the surface of Saturn's moons, but what
would be the value of such a simple conquest?
That's what they always asked in school.
It would be so restful but it would not be
the egg, that's plain enough. The egg
will have painted on it the blueprint
for a small blue man, and if
we don't find the egg, how will the man come forth?
But I myself have looked already

five million times under the clockstand,
among the vacant pillars of the bed and chair,
in the closet and in its every shoe and pocket,
and there's nowhere left except the porthole.
I follow you around the room
from one point of interest to another:
you leave small blue prints. And sometimes
we stop and wonder why the sun and stars
don't stop chasing themselves
endlessly around this vast egg we are in.

Exclusivity

Always too late you take the host and draw
a circle on the ground: but everything,
including Dracula's sisters, is inside.
And in some obscure sense is blest
by being there, though it seems simply to lie
inert, a desert of petrified closed hands.
Yet you are so disheartened, there rise up
only the beings who were to be left out:
a gangrenous head in a noose in the suburbs,
the atomic bomb growing in a breast,
a wino vomiting on your wife, and boys
throwing cats against walls. Here's where you start
to talk about beginning again, about
the eternal childhood of man, growing up this time
more in accord with the presentiments
of youth. Didn't they see this dusty rind
fading like hills in the lighted fog of morning,
a trick painting that disappears with age
to reveal the lovely one lost beneath?
Yet you too have lain on the ground crying
after the big guys beat you. This is,
as a matter of fact, your ageless portrait:
this fading world. Within it,
there being no other women and yourself
resolved against mirrors, the spilling into air,
you look more closely at one of Dracula's sisters.
A complete beauty seems to recall itself
in her eyes made yellow and full of broken edges
by a preternatural neglect. And like her, you
can see yourself now, a victim of the circle

that seeks to choose
but always is baffled by the fact
that there is one thing only. Now
she lifts her eyes again and after all these years
you recognize your cousin and your bride.

Because the Wind Went Over Us

Because the wind went over us, the sun,
passing to the south, warmed
the angle of the white stone wall
where you stood, looking toward the river.
In the green water the brick face of the tannery
across from us was eaten as though by moss.
A musty smell continually
slipped past with the November noon
in the wind. I think you were looking
farther up, where the white houses
glinted on the hill, chips of old snow
or flakes of dandruff in the frozen
tinder. Your presence is a selfish act,
of acceptance, of choosing what to take,
and the sirens screaming now and then
in the utter calm of these streets are like you.
Recalling the bonelike chill of that day,
I hardly know what I am. Those houses
in a neighborhood the sky carves out of diamond
hide men who live on equal terms
with competent wives. And yet they are
only your lovers, and so diffident
in this desire that their fear of you
is an unworthiness to live. You looked
far away. A box of the dried apricots
you're always eating was in your pocket.
The city is a kind of radiation
along which they want to come toward you,
as the eyes want to pass up the stream
of light to touch the sun
with their offering of knowing it.
By being afraid to ask, haven't those silent
men already killed you?
Their crime is to need so much.

Stabbing

We found you on the subway stair
struggling for breath, filled with twenty wounds,
blood fighting with the voice in your throat.
As the train had rattled forward
and left you there (progress
is the same as ever, but wrinkled now,
with falling teeth), it had happened
almost in silence in the passage upward
to night and the towers
that indicate and obscure the stars.
Twenty wounds: four times the number
of your senses, twice the number
of your body's natural openings. New doors
cut in you by a misery grown fierce
at what little it receives.

You were a symbol as he took you
and now are a girl dying.
Like so many other mutilations
done for the symbol's sake: lips
and foreskins mangled, false channels
opened inward, limbs and bodies
cut away in our desire
to conform to the red coming out
of day from night. And afterward we climbed
all night long past trees and clouds
till morning, the snow and blinding glare.
We were going to see god and redeem him
from the sacrifice he is said to need from us:
our enemy's heart, or a purchased girl
flung in the well, taking our daughter's place.
In the thin air our lungs were bursting
and the cold made us cry. We wanted
to consume pain without conceiving more,
to discover through long labor
the formula of transmutation.

And all this time in the city behind us
is your ordeal. The murderer
desperate to release the secret in you,
to make you speak and kiss
more deeply than your body tells him

is possible, to force a way in
for all that knocks and is not opened to.
Or so I say, trying to understand.
More simply I say he hated you
and wanted you to die. He could not see
what you are. And at once I desire
revenge, to commit on him what he has done,
inheritor of the centuries of false instincts,
rites founded on a mote in the eye,
the stupid illusion of evil. So the circle
reasserts its power: longing
to tear the miserable human things apart,
to drag knowledge from the beauty
that won't stop destroying itself.

Despite all effort continually in me
victim and murderer perform
all that was done in those dull lights underground.
In me without end, without physical sign,
the gift is also anger and a blow,
acquiescence is greed, possession
of cherished flesh is a wall.
The days eat amputations, the human body
digests its pain. And you now and he
are fragments in my mouth.

THE LAST THING

This dream is of doors open on streets
that twist away: canals filled solely
with the silver backs
of dolphins calling to be ridden,
ways drawn out of one another
through the intricate texture
of a jungle of glass and steel,
of fitted stones that change their color
with the angles of sunlight, windows
looking on vegetable interiors,
stairways of vine, furniture
of trees grown into the forms
the human body casts outward, decoration
of flowers and fruit, painted sculpture,
and mixed scents carving a shape

in the mind. And the whole city
shifts steadily, as it has brought
me here to you, or you to me,
again, and so will tear apart
and reunite us after further adventure,
as this fable plays at playing out
all its proliferating hopes.

Here we can love even those tales
in which a vague foreboding
takes a body of coincidental death,
even those myths that explain motionlessness,
a man and woman lying side by side
helplessly, as a mirror
explains death. What difference
does such a thing make—like a dry oak that seems
to dominate a plain full of scattered groves—
to whatever is condensing in this twilight
to pour itself over us
from the pitcher of morning? We will wake
and drink and go away separately
or together through the streets, winding down
toward another season of sleep, aware
each day in the late afternoon
of a nearly invisible rumor, a shadow
bearing a letter from the rim of the hills.
Nothing is forgotten, and this shape
darkens as it approaches us, at last
taking on substance at its entrance
into our bodies. The distant sounds
are remembered suddenly for the voices
of the disembodied, which they were
in the days before this incarnating sleep.
So we go on, always lightening, darkening,
in a secure and wild drama that once
in another life was reserved for the sky.

Analysis

I am an instrument
for the analysis of birds.
The feathers, removed,
are driven by the wind

into the earth's chest
covered with moss,
and in the woods the skeletons
continually cleansed and fouled
by rain endure,
by night rhyming and repeating
the moon in little circles of bone
on the muddy leaves. Of the flesh,
one part rots in me,
is dropped into the soil's
veins of sludge. The other is
converted to the motions
that make these curving marks
and to a faint heat
that moves out and out
with the stars
falling
where every direction is down.

The Problem

We have the problem here of changing life
as simply as different flowers knot the year,
invisibly, as out of August the snows grow usual.
Remember, last October when you were with us
we didn't believe that cold snap would never end,
was winter? And we were right, in a way.
The problem is that we change the things we say,
must change, with the bitter winds changing the woods
and spring's appearance in the first mild rain,
the unlocatable strangeness of our mornings.

It occurs that earth winds us up or out,
a spool not concerned with anything
and with nothing less than the dull line of thread.
Yet last night my sister dreamed of a vine
whose leaves were buses and buildings, drunks,
suburbanites, actors, Ohio, the Riviera,
Lake Chad, the oddly shaped patches that we've seen
of your life, and machines…all the disguises.
In the dream she knew, could prophesy,
strange associations the vine intended,

advancing underground like a new poetry:
how it would shoulder aside the heavy grains of dirt,
where it would fountain to light, in what corner
of the garden we'd never known before.

While this afternoon, again, sheep on the hillside
halfway up to the low, blinding overcast...
In this heat we name the time "waiting for rain."

And a catbird cries, invisible in the maple trees.

Fields in the Air

White flocks and shepherds are camouflaged
in a rolling down of cloud, fields in the air
that have opened to extend the light
in slanted roads to this mass.
Now I seem almost to remember...warriors there
would suddenly discover themselves to be:
whims of winter. And the young gods
would return from the boiling loam as crystal flowers
the first warm day, when the fountains are turned on.
And a hint descends of freedom
from the fear of being something else
besides oneself: it was to ride
the naked back of a huge horse fleeing
over the roofs of these houses that await
their poor winged fruit
to be born to their clicking trees.

Now I have rising feet, an urge to climb
onto an absence of routine, a shelf of rock
over residential valleys. But the light has come
not as a way but as a palm
that gently presses the body back in the grass
and slips as heat through the skin, becoming there
a gesture that struggles in clenched fingers.
The battle brings to the face a forgotten water.
Green shoots increase in the palm and force the hand.

Mansions

In the poor house the child's restlessness
moves him from bedroom to kitchen,
kitchen to living room, living room to bedroom.
He longs to have been born in mansions.
He's heard of libraries and studies,
conservatories, music rooms, verandas,
halls by which in the silence night,
water and the lawn and stars
and voices of the dead
penetrate a huge house like a skull
blown through by wind,
waiting for flesh
to return to it. He knows
rumors of windings, forkings,
passages leading to mistaken
unnecessary places
designed for no human use,
but put to unknown ends by someone:
the "phantom," who lived and died
unheard-of within the walls, content
that the owners mistook his movements
for mice or the creaking of dead boards.

So the child found the way outside. Here
nothing is banal, the most ordinary food,
when it is his, travels to the hand
in hands of the sun and rain,
and sleep is the night, and dreams
are objects grown shadows and the stars.
Is it only, then, the habit
of a hard childhood
that he enters every thicket,
lifts every rock, parts every waterfall,
looking for a door?

It's unclear to him, like the dazzling
mystery of this palace entered
and deserted continually by signs.
If he tries to follow them
there is nowhere they can have gone,
nowhere else to go: their source
and resting place must be hidden somewhere here.

And he too begins and ends here,
like the flash and whistle of a bird,
his only house the undivided weather.

AMONG WHITE BUILDINGS

Among the white buildings here, the problem
that stirs you and dissolves
is to speak of this architecture
that makes art of simple motion along the walks.
Moving among towers, the eye draws
from sky and hills cut and reshaped
by the rooflines a liquid body:
continuous like a cloud,
one but never the same. Or say
that the towers are plants with seeds that dream
when and what they will; their flowers
may burn for a season, or wink and die.
Or say that, riddled with eyes like wounds,
they are heads of buried giants whose thought
is flesh and who when morning strikes them
sing men and women.
                          Endless are the ways
it might be said. This September noon,
the sun at its height, slightly away to the south,
in the cold wind all possible lives
pierce to this spot and touch a sense
within the senses: not only the leaf
too far-off in the crown of a distant oak
to be distinguished, but past and future leaves.
And people flash through the walls
of masonry and time, conduct their wars
and wash their dishes here, in space
that you would once have sworn these trees
and this sun-checkered openness possessed alone.
Just so a chord is of all instruments,
yet each the light shows us as an object
seeming silent within its sphere.

Before the Eyes of Statues

How many useless prayers
have we performed
before the eyes of statues,

while the homunculus
who loves you,

whom I raise each night
and augment in my own image,

is wasting in his cell?

Romance

There are houses I love looking at: gray stone,
which trees surround and which sweat water
in dreary weather like the rocks near a falls.
The upper stories seen from a block away
through gaps in the leaves are ruins, and on the roof
the air in winter presses with the same
weight and captured hues as ice. And if
you stand up there behind the balustrade,
the lidless slit of the bay must stare
into your eyes, and a dull gleaming that rhymes
faintly with the snow in the dim street
curls around your ankles. But the huge elm
that hangs above you at last forgets
its black scratching on a crumpled paper
and becomes a head again. You see up now
through intricacies, out past an avalanche
of green hair to blue pieces of some other place.
Though this house wraps gleams of polished glass
around itself, through the transparent cloth
still it reminds you of a face the way
a woman's body does: a face
with one expression, a round-mouthed gaze,
that seems about to utter a long formless sound.
But when a man with a Great Dane opens
the door and leaves, he is an idea
materializing in the form of fruit
on its tongue. It is this man, the owner,

who in September sits in the curved turretlike
third-story study above the lake.
A mass of strings from his radio is a current
that rushes him under the phosphorescent roof
of a low tunnel underground. The foghorns
and the clank of railroad cars fall through
his windows the way accidents create music.
It seems that huge chunks of rock tumble behind him
and change in falling to birds and flying reptiles
of hollow and tinted blown glass: they ring
like half-drunk glasses of water touched
by silver rods. He goes to sleep
and is cast up where the sun pulls roses
from the carpet. All day passing over,
it calls on different corners: the stags running
on the stairway wall, a fierce table
holding stones in its claws. At noon the old
lady sealed in flannel and the girl
in her jersey bathing suit sit like clothes
thrown over chairs in the garden. Narcissus
in the birdbath stoops, a centerpiece,
displaying how he hangs more fragilely
than a leaf, though made of stone. And soon
they're asleep, I forget how the house reminds me
of water streaming from a stone carving
in cold rain. I approach the wrought iron gate
for a better view of the garden. And now the owner
with his black dog comes back around a corner
and shouts, "What do you want here?" What I want
is like this never to be finished looking.
What I want is poetry like this house.

MEMORIES OF A SMALL TOWN CHILDHOOD

The horizon always seemed to you and me
too big a word to mean those dirty rooftops
pasted against a gray newspaper of sky
so wet the print ran down all over us.

Remember how we would stay inside in bed?
Far below us the blue carpet crawled,
flecked with tiny ships, an amber light
flowing over it among the silhouettes

of columns. Wasn't that when our earthly parents
smiled silently
and with a loud bang our favorite willow,
the green tent of our heavenly parents' hair,
caught fire and disappeared
in the direction of the sky? And then a net
fell from it over you and wrapped you up
and suddenly you looked to me like a pear
made by a spider out of spit and flies.

But before, we did nothing all day long but breathe
and receive visitors, remember? Or armies
of your fellow girls would follow us
blindly through head-high grass
into the sweet ambush of singing frogs, of night
and the smell of water.

Now they tell me that you are starving
and I trust them: they command the food
and why should they give you any?
After all, you don't touch anyone here,
there is no necessity in you, the walls
are bulging and the stairway has fallen down
entirely without you.

The Blue Gardenia

Removing her watchwork cape, the woman
who has ceased to menstruate
goes down to the riverside.

Fernlike, the black glass buildings
close behind her. In darkness, in dream
seeing her, you are afraid

of night, afraid of sleep.
By her womb that betrays her,
do you know her?

Now she has come to the old Ford
that waits on the river road.
And it glides with her to the ruined shell

of the Blue Gardenia on its cliff
above the sea. The sea shakes
the rotten walls like a desperate man

pounding on a door. It is again
a certain night that slowly you recall:
November 1939, in the period of the moon's dark,

when you felt her senseless blood
pulse into the blood-colored,
endlessly deep carpet

of Bert Milonzi's rooms
back of the gaming hall...
her little chrome revolver smoking,

his smashed shoulder, his good hand
like the jaws of a factory crane
on her arm, and the broken bottle

that was scraped across her wrist: so little pain.
A warming rush goes through her
and dies within her as a man dies...

Like tides, the constant ebb
of this recurring climax
mocks her and the child within her.

In minutes the torpedoes
of Sheriff Ed Greer arrived. His vow
was kept: to make her a betrayal,

the excuse for cleaning out Milonzi
and throwing the roulette wheels
into the sea. Milonzi slumps

bleeding in the white
Cubist chair, watching
like deserted binoculars

the mouthless smile
of her dying, and her gold lamé,
the metallic skin that had seemed to her

more beautiful than her own flesh.
She is laid on the billiard table. Greer,
the gambler knows, has taken over his county,

he is a dead man. And Greer
laughs, watching the final
drops seep out of her

as if he had come across
a drink spilled in an empty room.
She scarcely notices

when she fades past the screaming
of the tuxedos and evening dresses
and the sheriff standing,

a civic statue in the yellow light.
And now after many years white starlight
enters through the roof of a ruin

to play in the bottomless eyes
of rats and owls. The old moon seems
to set into this broken building:

this is the place where the moon is
on those nights when there is no moon.
And your end, her end, is always playing here:

the gunfire contention that infects
the invisible slimness of the resting moon
with its next month's pregnancy and death.

In this late fall the overgrown garden
of the abandoned nightspot is a forest
of whips, palisades and clubs.

You are stiff, sitting in the Ford. It has stopped,
hands open the car door and your steps lead you,
lolling like a hypnotist's subject,

up the crushed gravel walk,
and bring your swelling body to the place
where its shadow and its child will melt away.

A shot. A broken bottle. And you are laid
on the waiting billiard table. The gray clouds
are rushing again tonight across the glassless

windows of this split husk resembling
the hull of a ship on rocks. The starlight
reflected between your breasts is a white flower:

you are dead. The journey to birth
of the empty blue hull begins.

Deaf as a Post

November served a flower to the tide
which followed into a tunnel where an abolished country
sang softly to the tiny corpse of its language:
"You too are called upon to suffer, to decline and die."
The red flower
was pulled apart by red nails and sealed in an envelope
where all that has been severed or disconnected
is on its way to some address.
Everything: farms that burn and laugh
because they are only dirty windows
through which wheat and profit watch each other with longing
and make clumsy signs.
Bushes of razors clinging to a windy slope.
Dust prepared by horns, served on the shattered trays
of the servant of a hundred broken arms.
Even women who invite us to stay for dinner
and astonish and dismay us
with their desperation.
And now an uprooted signal,
surviving the death of the impulse that gave it birth,
is carried along the street in a leather sack,
or higher, rides in a needle
that wounds and stitches the sky with smoke.
Folded upon itself, this message: ignorant,
far removed from the superior nature of language,
and in fact totally asleep,
not even dreaming of the power of a young girl
whose arm pierced the earth to create it
only yesterday, rising up through rock
to mark this shore,
to destroy idly with horrible pain a red flower.

Triumph of Epicurus

Long before the discovery of tomatoes
the poets chanted that he is an idiot who does not know
the world is a tomato over which a horse is galloping.
This they sang till it came to the ear of Epicurus
who arose and murdered them with his foot.

"Let America," he said, "rot in the wave,
apple of love and discord. Let France
remain unborn, where madness bleeds from the eye.
Seeking freedom, imagination creates these monsters.
But each thing and the whole world is obedient to law
and the gods are powerless, as we aspire to be.

"For if things were created out of nothing, the octopus
would be born of this horse, and in winter a harvest
of springless clocks might bow down and crush the pear trees.
Nor would anything await the hour of its dissolution
but one would see the bridegroom turn to powder
and another man seize the bride, wiping the dead from her shoes."

So he spoke. Yet what is Athens now?
Only a white fire in a blue grave.
Fish scour the Pantheon
where a marble torso wields a scepter that cries.
And the thoughts of Epicurus when at midnight
with closed eyes he made his dream from the things that are,
his burning needle with its thread of smoke,
his garment of the valleys and days—

all is dispelled,
and perhaps one atom of all his atoms
enters into this delirium I sing against the wall.

Aesthetic Distance

Winter separates beauty and luxury.
The setting sun, a reminiscence of power,
nests in the bony groins of the trees.
Blue shading to the dusky gray
of ash swallowing embers: the color

of the wall where openings blaze.
And you look at those windows, a dead man
keeping his distance.

Why attempt to reclaim a life
that is now far-off?
It would slip from the hand again,
or through this hand, these arms,
powerless to touch or hold. You'd watch
from the top of a tall staircase
your crying son embrace your shadow
three times, three times pass through it
and it walk on as if asleep.

What would it be in silence
to sit by your son's fire unwarmed,
to move yourself closer until he sees you
throned in the blaze, burning
but never burnt, shivering in flames?
Soon enough he'll know the loins
for banners the wind erodes,
leaving at last only the silver pole.

Better to subsist on beauty
though a desire to desire recurs,
a desire to wring a note from absent bowels
of the organ under absent leaves.
But you are kin to what endures,
the little, the bone beneath,
and the greed of the childish wifely flesh
once gone, you are restored. Rising,
the sun drives a tide of fleeing
blood up the polished limit
of what you can see; a little later
the winter day revives, pale,
an effortless whiteness peopled
with essential forms and the exact
traveling of slow shadows.
Day and night there is nothing
not your own to trouble you,
and no fullness that, bursting the vessel,
makes an end
to the meal of contemplation.

Modern Love

It is so refining
its heat drifts far from the fire.

There it is: a locked room mystery
with the millionaire as if asleep
in his deep black chair. It hangs above
the snow on your roof,
a fire-banded chestnut
above the lightly swelling breasts of the snow.
It is a freezing moon most like
Alexandria's last word
examining her learnèd smile
in the hot bottom of a cloud.

Do you mind being its huge confusion?
The way the light hair of the trees, which grow
downward from the sandy sky, falls
into your mouth. The absences
of their buried faces and slim trunks.
And as far above you as stars,
the wet groins of their limbs.

The teenage party of their wind
blows down to you and licks you all over
with the powder puff of conversation.
You are so beautiful then, a lime pastel.
You know what this is preluding:
the guillotine is visible in the square
through the instruction sheet
that serves love's antique haberdashery as door.
Love sees the cart bearing its head away.
Thus grows the visible like a bourgeois soap.

It is so cleansing
the need to see it washes far from your eyes.

On the Bluff

We walked together to the bluff,
stood on a level with faint clouds,
were words on the tip of a tongue

about to be spoken, thrown
out over the water
to seek in the comprehension
of someone unknown a new body.

We must go separately. I want
only to turn back with you,
walk back through the crumpled tongues
crackling around our ankles, hands
of cold water
clutching our legs on the beaches.
You remember the gate
between the willow and the poplar?
On this side were the rising paths
in the waste field where we lay:
crickets and flies, a small pool,
wild wheat and hollow milkweed;
on that side, the houses
fanned by the rows of trees.

We were praying, then, for the sky
to demand nothing,
to imprison for us
that moment and leave us free.
If time would stop,
we would have time enough
to wander through and love
all that now keeps passing with us,
dying elsewhere, unknown.

Its pain penetrated our sleep.
We awoke. The lake crawls
far below us here and opposite
are the vague signs. You are saying,
"Leave me.
Don't leave me here to die."

The Ground

1

Now your body
is the forest you wander through,
never encountering a limit.

There's no one here. You meet
an eye balancing on a nerve, looking up,
an ear that bows itself to the moss,
a bush of hands, unmoving lips
clinging to tree trunks.

Are there people nearby, concealed
behind the screen of air?

They own plots for temples here
but no one comes to build.
No conversation. Formless areas
to be entered: sleep and waking,
night and shade.

You roam the streets of a blueprint
inscribed in the white ground.
Only ferns rise,
suggesting it, hiding it.

2

The clay fragment of a wall
on which the plan was written
in a language you don't know:

"...in him
and he in you..."

Do you remember it,
was it something you found one day
and forgot, only to think of now?

Or did a dream construct it
from desire?

A ruin drops a seed. Or a stone
where no one but the accidental wind
has scratched a note
builds in you,
in the form of a ruin
overgrown with moss and vines,
the idea of a temple.

But the stars
and the spaces among stars
are only an ear
and you are the sense of hearing:

aroused by this hint, perfectly still,
you strain within yourself
for a city, a people,
a voice that is not raised.

3

Something goes through the world
continually raising and letting fall
the voice, the hammer, the glass of wine.

From far away, it is a man
dreaming underneath a tree.
Approaching, you enter
a city where all the walls
are doors open. Music
is synonymous with night.

As shade waters the light,
talk waters quietness.
Night and day succeed.

The maple tree sees the gleam
of a sleeper preparing for bed
in a house's eye. The wood
and stone tell each other
"good night" and both are seeds
of a dream that prepares itself
within the sleeper.

The corridor of morning air
opens on a work site
where the worker reaps diamonds
from his brow.

They purchase the opening
of flowers in a season of fruit.

4

A bone tinkers with a watch,
turning it back
before hands, before metals,
before number and time.

The bone smiles.
An old woman's smile
to the young is always half malign:
sunlight on western windows,
water falling.

But the bone will tell you
it wants to be a girl again
as always: perfectly young,
perfectly naked and unafraid.

A huge form
that does not live as living men
will come again and remind her,
"This is how men live."

A wind blows the ground
from under your feet
into a dark box. You bequeath
whatever will remain of you
to silence and night.

But a rumor of talk keeps playing
from the midst of the disaster.
And out of the faint hubbub
your own voice turns
from the other voices a moment
and asks you,
"What do you think you are?"

In the night, laughter and rags
of music from the house
step out into the spaces
under the wet trees.

5

Come out of the forest,
where you have buried yourself.
Here are the figures
that give you its leaves for hands.

Do not be angry with me
that I am married now.
In a dream I fell
back past the cage of lashes
and bodies split at the joints.
I fell into this bed
with what seemed a motion of ascent.

In the garden are ears to hear you,
eyes to see, lips to respond.
The strings of your ears and eyes
and brain will grow proportionate.

You stand in the breast of a dead man.
But I preceded and I follow you
and it is only the earth
covered with moss.
The social roots build there,
drawing from all directions
fruit and flower that decide
with sap of the unbidden emissaries.

The threat is made of fear.
Nothing is idle, not even
a rock lying in an airless chest.

6

Voices
conversing nonchalantly
about what is...
Who's speaking? Where
is that celebration?

Absence is your trousseau,
the tuxedo of the spouse.

But the spouse has taken you,
you are together
where those voices are, while here
still you see silent things alone.

Your intercourse is only
two sentences, motionless,
naked side by side:

"We are together here."
"Where are you?"

Everything is completed
and you wait,
because you don't find the way,
no one comes to find you.

And someone else,
scarcely moving, says, "I am
in wood, in water...
Slip into my breast,
be lost in me."

But you don't hear him. Still
waiting for someone lost,
you say, "I am the ground—
inhabit me."

Under Crossed Swords

Yours, custodian of health,
are the dark roots,
and it is yours to make them walk,
white feet that shine in the stream,
hardly bend the grass
and one day will not bend it.

No vein attaches you
to the heart, the belly.

You severed the fleshy line
to release yourself,
to move past the tattered weeds,
the rotting vegetable
lifted on the swell.
Yet still a constellation
draws blood up to your body.

The things spilling
out of the motionless gorge
grow small in your eyes.
We were in a dream, were disgusted,
but it spit us out and now
we see it,
the gem in our ring:

as we saw that swollen spider
on a trellis of morning glories
and then walked back
under crossed swords in leaf.

Dark Pocket

At night faint winds
are collecting papers
in the hedge. Gleaming,
rosewood beetles move and stop
under marigolds.

Strengthless fingers
are fumbling in this dark pocket
for a match,
for a key.

In the Maligned Museums

In the maligned museums the people live,
if more slowly than we do. The watchman
is no more to them than a white cone
of flashlight that picks its way
as carefully as a drunken man.

The watchman thinks, "My look creates
these scarabs crawling on the painted
breasts of wood princesses, these bullets
that have already killed their man,
these singular animals which are
the collected flotsam of whole races."

The watchman's nervous look creates
motion in the eyes of the tyrannosaur,
a warm hand on the mace raised to fall,
the incredible disappointment of a tomb
opening to release a corpse armed
as a proselyte of decomposition.

But more like Paris in the nineties,
one of those eddies that introduce
the flat sea surface to its depths,
the museum gathers after business hours.
Only the watchman creeps, leery of strange death.

THE UNDERGROUND

A poet who fought against occupying forces during World War II responds to the criticism that, because his work stands for freedom in his now totalitarian country, he is encouraging the enemy and thus inviting nuclear war.

Where is the world that lives? I've seen
the metal nipples measuring out
exact excretions of ground meat
into little cans...and the cattle
chained so that they can't move,
because they have been bred for so much flesh
and so little bone, to move
might break the pelvis, spoiling the meat:
so many, a whole race of fat
in an infinite corridor of stalls,
dropping dung on one conveyor,
eating continually from another.

I remember when the tanks passed through here,
crushing the hedges, ignoring the roads
already drawn through the orchards, the vineyards,

smashing the grapes—to make
a wine of misery—into the soil.
And in the gaps between the tanks, the men
with submachine guns and flame throwers
to fill out the solid advancing line
of death.

And yet they passed like ghosts:
through us, terrifying us, sending us
to bar ourselves in our houses,
carrying off many to the dead;
strengthless nonetheless, ineffectual,
a presence desperate to repossess
body and blood but consigned to shadows
and the conquest of shadows.
They made a shadow of the day
and tried to seize us there. But it was we
who disappeared, our world that vanished
during the day into calm villages
that made bread, composed prayers to Hitler,
saw their inhabitants taken.
Then at night we were in the hills
and existed once more, a dream world
that was abolished in the blinding shadow dawns
and rose again each dusk. And we
passed through the conqueror, as the living
pass through the dead.

No city was ours, no plain of farms,
no lines of tracks or wires
across the mountains. We held
no bridges over the rivers, no ships
or ports. The microscope and telescope
were theirs, the radio, the offices full of records,
the road and the trucks. And still
I wrote and my friends read, the words
scratched on cheap re-used papers
or repeated from camp to camp
in the caves where the fires were hidden.
How the absence of desks, of schools,
of many books, swelled our memories.
The words took the place of towns and fields.
So we would strike, and they
would cry, "Where is this world?"

finding another heap of their gray brothers
uniform, motionless, flecked with living blood
as if partially redeemed.
Solid bodies, men of flesh
we stood among them, untouchable.

This has happened. Yet they tell me
that words—which demand the people
should have what is theirs and was stolen,
should have it now—
must mute themselves lest these walls
be broken up and the fragile plant,
poetry, be the first to die.
If fire covers the whole earth
we will write, until the poison
invisible in the water
dissolves our bones. Our children
will write until the scales
bind their wrists, and the thumbs
drop from their hands grown claws.
We will read until the air eats our eyes
and then listen, remember, recite. Among us
the city will be built,
will spread from the speaker's lip
to the ear of the listener. Perhaps
no human hand will ever again
touch stone with power, but in the word
even the dead who invented death will rise.

THE SMOKER

The effigy of the smoker
floats over the corner:
a black sun, this enormous girl
drawing white smoke, a strand
of vacuum, out of space
into the weave of air and human lungs.
And in the female trinity
of her eyes and smile,
now you follow the single thread
into the flowering almonds
that flame before the doors,
into the miasma of perfume, lake of sleep,

into grateful wood, metal rescued from objects,
rocks that catch fire in the blaze of a winter midnight,
the cemetery of erect water and leaf-bearing lamps,
children whistling in the branches,
a red jaguar
drawing a white stripe through the eye,
exhausted cattle in a May shower of heated lead,
cheap books on health and deviation,
eaten faces,
a girl's small treasure in its pouch,
raccoons in the attic and on the wooded hill...
all the juice, the glint, the clamor of the day
poured over gray rocks, tinted green by the ferns,
asleep in its traditional wound
in a new light between coins and a blank wall.

WITH SATISFACTION

It was a beautiful day after all.
A sleek syllable
flew from your mouth—a bird
of middling size and modest beak,
with bright plumage
but such as blended well
with the somber firs.
A conclave of tiny white forms
on a gray background,
the small stones at the lake's edge
suggested one another, moistened
by the lip and tongue of the water.
The man just down the way
caught many fish,
far more than your father did:
he would live a much longer time.
The slamming of doors
had already begun to tell you
that you would not live long,
and that nevertheless you would want,
now and then,
to die before you can.
That day
there was just one fish for you—
and you looked at it
with satisfaction.

Stranded

Your lunch hour is an island
ringed with scattered shade of sparse trees,
as far as a lonely shepherd in a bad painting
from the office towers that bend over
and peer through gaps in the leaves.
The complaints of a dozen kinds of birds
and the coughing of trucks along
the invisible freeway
blend to a background for a nearer music:
one yellow-jacket
working in a bush.
But look out: now he's mistaken
your brightly colored tie
for a flower. And now
he's alighted purposefully on the knot
right next to your throat.
Stand as still as you can, just swaying
slightly, naturally in the light gusts...
but how long can you continue to fool him?
The bell for one p.m. will ring
and you'll have to move,
he'll be undeceived and you
will be a dead man. Already angered
by his fruitless search
among bogus petals, he'll strike...
unless perhaps you stay here like this,
scarcely moving, forever,
closing your eyes to the moon,
staring at the sun.

Diana

So you are lying in the tall wild grass
and the stalks that neighbor those your body
crushes cut you a coffin lid of sky:
a coffin the shape of your body
extends above you to where the light
presses its blue seal down. The horizon of this world
is as near you as the limits of your form. Above it,
straws in her knotted black hair, straws
and dirt and crushed ants in the sweat drying

on her breasts, she stands up now, awake.
The pressure of the ground has made her buttocks red,
has traced there with weeds and pebbles a webwork
of canals and craters. The black eyes
don't shine but occupy with a predatory
want one side of the sky as the sun slides down
the other. Her body, which men call "white," is
a nameless color in which everything relaxes.
Her knee breaks through a curtain of your grave
and she stretches upward in a huge X.
You seem to remember a time when the cold moisture
glinting on her legs was warm. Her face
is lax and the grass blades stand around her:
it's Diana, at last rising from the field.

Episode from North American Folklore

Even stranger that you thought is the hermit,
a true giant, who lives in a cave near here.
People shudder and cross themselves at his traces:
huge tracks; remnants of a brief moment of filth
at the edge of town behind the Quonset huts
in his life like a fresh snowfield; occasional motions
at midnight in the corners of eyes,
like pieces of the dark shifting and melting away;
and in the morning blood on a cracked fence post.
His presence is a cover for every child abductor
and chicken thief in these mountains. But his thoughts,
now that perhaps he has forgotten human language,
sitting so many years in his cave full of bones:
are they like a silent film?
Or a glass of water spilling? What shape
does his time take—none but the alternation
of snowstorm, and blinding glare, and the stars?
I ask merely to give you something to think of
tonight when, the wife and children sleeping, a glass
of brandy in the colorless ticking silence
feels like a club in your hairless palm.

The Katoliko

These four sweet rivers flowing
from the ruined hopes of the distant baptized
water my kingdom. They bring fertility
that fosters age, a rich bottom of the past,
silt in which memories sprout spontaneously,
from no seed, and grow rank.
Who knows whether this crop has any roots
or begins simply at the surface of the ground,
whether anything in this kingdom of remains
was ever whole? Geon and Fison,
Tigris and Euphrates, how well hidden
is your common headland.
To all other countries a garden to the eastward,
Runculat it afflicts with its presence. Armies,
citizens, peasants, beggars, the very dogs
beneath the tables are indolent
with the nearness of a hope that does not dispense itself.
Standing by the river or ankle-deep by the banks,
they watch the leaves and fish drifting down
and look upstream. Here and there among them
is one of the foolish metal men, a king maybe
or duke in his own country, who also feels
these waters flow from a place he has deserved.

Nativity

Seldom except in the apple orchard night
where mint composes the seventh proof
is an answered granted to fear.

Cities where the cancer eats through a throat
and leaves a second hungrier mouth,
the seneschal is singing a comic song
among comic retainers and dogs
knee-deep in bones in the drafty hall.
And if we leave now, forever
the hero will be suspended from a rope
and the unstaunched tears of the maiden
will flood the streets.

There is nothing in the world but stars
hung above miraculous births
where the cows for a moment are touched with intelligence.
And the few bearers of gifts
are desperate with poverty, ignorance and lack of time.
If they never reach you, recall
that to have you we let the woman betray us
with the pit of our own sleep.

CATALOGUE OF BOURGEOIS OBJECTS

Candle in the form of a white numeral 1 with a green monkey on its back
Statuette of bisexual Siamese twins, the base of the passive's throat joined
    to the dominant's crotch, her nose melting into his navel
Victorian lady and gentleman of black yarn hung by their collars
Four shepherds and four shepherdesses on a mahogany plain with a flock of
    hardened gum drops
Frightened hailstorm that attempts to return to the sky
Pond of vertical surface clogged with chartreuse plaster, several light
    switches, half of an oak door
Painting of an inverted tulip with a clipped stem touching the keyboard of a
    rusty shadow
Pair of toilets with blue fur, trained to eat table scraps
Silver tray full of dried tongues (with miniature broadsword)
Three-footed wingless bird of prey with desolate plateau head dominated by
    the following obsession: a naked woman balancing a blank head on her
    blank head, the topmost head wearing a hat which is a burning mainsail
One reedless clarinet among a rattling of dried reeds
Passageway that prevents the rain from touching you
Discreet cupboard which has endured many dinners without ever giving its
    untainted service
Wicker stand full of promises
Several ghosts, singly and in assorted groups, who bear striking resemblance
    to their former bodies at certain appropriate moments (each with gold
    safety leash)
Fishbowl with fish of purple waxen balls and the scent of vaudeville lilacs
Fire in which magic log burns without being consumed
Several shrines consisting of cavelike apertures fenced with steel net, where
    dry heat issues from below
Mary with God's only sibling, a tired vine, struggling from her belly
Sacred book wherein you are reminded to plant in the spring
Star that will descend from the night sky when you want to read
One inexhaustible fund of variations on certain themes, chiefly that crime
    does not pay

One room of furniture for a pet dwarf
Birdbath with attached birds of various plumage and in various postures
    of delight
Leafless tree where melodramas roost
Mechanized guillotine with procession of haughty blades
Decorative thicket of shy virgins succeeded by dragons
One small fortune in petrified eyeballs
Glass-eyed cabinet of further silence
Rivers of orange flowers everywhere
Six cascades of drummer boys and milkmaids
Statue of the sun with a clock in his womb

THE VOICES IN THE AIR

The voices in the air, passing again
into earth, contract to drop that gleam
on plants or barren tracts. On the patio
eyes open above a book. There comes a sound
of scratching at softened wood.

Beyond the screen, twilight creates its bower
in the garden where not a leaf is whole.
Nothing but eaten shapes, robbed numbers;
and if absently you broke a twig,
an old friend might speak again in pain
from the wound pouring sap into the night:
a root begging you for your aimless feet.

And the wilderness goes on spreading,
strengthless tendencies rebounding everywhere,
watery echoes flowing into hollows.
A tireless breathing approaches on littered paths.
Listening, fearful, you pray some god
to hide you, root and leaf, in the earth.

But how soft the air is now,
the sky on the boundary of blue and gray.
Silence: only the bats dislodged by twilight
into their zigzag hunger
emit small shrieks: the remains
of a word called back by friends
who went still farther, too far.

Between the Root and the Flower

A Narrow Silent Throat

How many nights eaten by rain
have I sat here, dreaming of the world,
this world which is, facing a blank wall,
the sound of ruining water?

Or dreaming by day when dust
filled the throat and the dry light
burnt all strength from the eyes:
a dream of night with its grateful moisture
out of the sides of the air,
its repose of trees and hedges, its gift
of music in running water?

Dreaming in suffocating nights
of a noon on wooded slopes:
breathable flame, agate that quenches thirst,
and the excellent shape of a maple leaf,
its shadow among a million shadows
conferring a just degree
of darkness upon day: the vegetable
humanizing the light.

Dreaming of a life still possible
in an anguished moment,
a narrow silent throat
where one by one, pulsing and shining,
the unbodied elements pass.

The Window

You are the window so vast and clear
the whole house is dissolved in transparency.
The stones are melted away,
fused in a glass that is the end
of all blemish and the shame of matter.
The bricks are glass, the glass is air,
the air is light. And we are among the things we see,
at liberty in the heart of each thing,
in every cell of mineral or flesh.
You who divide me from what I watch
lead me to it and unveil it,

bind me to its breast and find for me
in the dark far beneath eyes and hands
its secret entrance.
You deliver me up: looking through you
I am naked where the only color is light,
where the wind of the moon's passing
shifts the mountains of granulated ice;
and still further, where the sole beings
are absolute zero and lightlessness.
Yet you are a window
and back of you is this study
where at peace the watcher sees himself
lost and found in the nonhuman things.

IN YOU THE SUN

In you the sun rises and sets,
days fall into evening and night,
the air grows violet and opaque.

Crickets, squirrels and parliaments
are asleep in a huge room, preparing
for the guest who will uncover what is lost.

And in winter sundown, you see,
framed against the blue wash grading to rose
of the west, a bleached tree stir.

Your skin is the distant walls of houses
watched by a cold being crouched
in wet fields at night. What you call

darkness, wind and the cleave of thunder
are effects of his voice that stretches
towards you through stillness,

crossing vacant lots. He is nothing
that you know of and his constant speech
lies around you helplessly as water.

Witness to Dusk

We were witnesses: it was the man
who lost color first, before the sky,
and gave the example to night.

Leaning at the rail as if straining
to fall into the gray water,
the man transformed himself
to a cowl, its back turned, filled
with who knows what—seaweed or broken rock.

It was not the sky. The clouds
at first made gaudy resistance.
But the dark imperial figure escaped itself,
flowing beyond its contour
as though it were nothing but a new blood
come to claim the body of what we saw.

Then we first noticed that in our frames
the beat of the engines transmitted from the deck
disguised itself in perfect time with our pulse-beats,

and that from their power
the motionless sea was fleeing.

Bell

Even the transparent bell of ice
around me, whose tongue I am,
which blurs the images
of all those others I recall
from the single childhood
that was ours...even this
might melt in the paternal
glance that sweats sweet water
from the green tongues.

O fade its heavy toll
from imperial absences that stalk among
driven snows of green wings and tatters,
ghost light that tries to eat
but the food falls through its hollow body

into the stream. Lift it from the perfumes,
those wax fingers on the door
of your high furnace.

Then this weight swinging
will still in its gone shell and hear
all those guests whose thin appeals
echo there in your hall,
around your placeless table.

Loud Light and Quiet Light

Loud light and quiet light,
nights filled with chaos
and nights of emptiness... There was a power
emerging from behind our skulls
to make a blue insistent fire, as cool
and still as a frozen eye,
of some blank thing: maybe a tiny stone
wounding our feet. We lay inert
in that force which, working through, made
of the same dying bee, its drone
in a warm day crossed by frigid veins,
an inexhaustible chamber
and a meager sign, a half-voiced word
falling
from decayed lips, imitating
by its obscure descent what it would say.
How is it that one day redeems the world
and the next throws it into hell, which a moment ago
could not exist in a universe too benign?
How without moving,
without having any hands,
did you and I lay hands on the world and move it,
so that the cricket gaily preached
unrepeatable truths that will never come again
from its perch on an old stove half submerged
in the stream? Or grasshoppers rose
into the light and like arrows
shot to tall flowers and fastened there
while something resembling a human body,
brown and soft, dropped
from a twisted apple tree into mud.

This world, aloof from us, where we two are
the most helpless, the most motionless
of all the particles, our eyes
pools of water where the flat sky comes
to curve, to rejoice,
turn to nothing, and cry.

September

Without strength or anger a bee
buzzes in my hand: already
somewhere there are queenless hives
and disheartened torpor among these beings
with no knowledge and no sadness.
In the light of this noon already
a crystal splinter, seed
of marvelous ice, begins to stir.

On the hill the pods are open: fountains of flax,
the drops rising and floating off to fall
elsewhere, far away. And the hill is flecked
with bright gashes, with colors of the bruise,
yellow and heavy brown. The waves of goldenrod
break around Queen Anne's Lace, each flower
a stretched palm with its purple central wound
a coin for the sky's persuasion.

September vanishes. But in me
nothing will ever change. It is the same
voice that mutters over the gaps,
the empty spaces many guests have left.
And though others succeed, always more,
no place is filled. The final
flares of the months burn
their absences into me.

Oak Branch

Always I carry with me a dead oak branch
with its inert hanging flames,
leaves the color of tarnished copper.
And in the dusk I light it as a smoky torch

at the candle of a woman not yet old,
abandoned by her lover years ago,
who still waits nightly for his return
whether from death, animal joy, or fear of her new life.

Now she is on the verge: her love and tenacious sorrow
will soon be habit, her devotion a mild insanity.
Children will make of her and this room,
where already she begins to collect tiny figures,
a superstition, a darkness
in the too plain light of the gridlike neighborhood.
She will grow white and fat, seldom venturing out,
and the neighbors will think of her as legend,
listening to her endless soft complaint about the mails:
they will feel a ruin speaks, a worn stone,
which has been crossed by power in other times,
which bears some obscure markings
but now it is inert in the banal day.

Today she is still beautiful and not yet old.
She leaves her candle burning each night
and falls asleep staring at the flame.
In the morning awakening: intricate pattern of the brocaded quilt,
infinitely regular, where eye and mind lose themselves.
And common motions: substances pressing on the tongue,
whistles entering the ears, a stirring almost of fingers
on the bare arm and from beneath, from within,
a mindless pressure in the throat.
White as with too much radiance, too much heat,
is all she sees: the rich colors in the cool shaded room.
Light: a strong god, creator of transparency and dust.

Dead wood, dead fiber, dead flesh,
and the midst of it this beauty, mesmerized,
or like a man awakening after a stroke
in a new world where nothing moves,
where the will bites itself to death or shoulders its pack
and turns round with the hours.
I don't know what has happened to her, where she is going,
what care prompts her to reach back from so far away
and nightly light her candle.
But a fire kindled there lasts a long while.
Sometimes at dawn the dead branch is still burning
and its leaves like a spray of stars light up the noon.

Dark Man

I am the dark man, so dark
that in shadow or memory you would say
my flesh grows green.
When the light flickers under towering
oaks and willows, it seems to you that light
pierces me also, that there are blue
spaces in my chest and deep in me
a quivering, an unseen rushing, and a family
of chaotic notes shot with quick rhythms and melodies.
I too, like the lawn in the park,
have my tones of liquid ash and gold
that move across me. And sometimes at the end
of a lane of trees I seem to walk
into noon's darkly striped face as a suicide
fades into the bright sea.
Or if you stay close to me till evening,
you will lose me then, when you turn to look
at the mounded black and orange clouds
lying in the west at the field's edge
above the heads of the trees. You notice I am gone
but at once your question is lost in other questions:
what is the source of night, does dark gather
and mount from the hedges, from basements,
the woods, the interiors of spruce; or does it fall,
does shadow fall, this shadow as large as the earth...
and what is it to be deprived of light?

And when you are with me, you wonder at the source
of my wealth and my idleness. A sound
of running water at my feet reminds you
of gardens under harsh suns, Provence, Palestine
or Africa. You think of a wine farmer,
nobles of Sicily, an ancient house
where the last son oversees a green remnant
of former holdings. A man with nothing to do,
keeping to his shade and his streams
in a dusty country, where villages of dust cling
to mountains of dust and the people
sit staring at white walls: the street, the land, the sky.
A man who has learned all languages, knows
all literature and music, studies the stars
and writes without signing the work.

Yet for all this you confuse me in your thought
with an idea of the field, wild grass in motion
sprinkled with mustard flowers and apple trees.
And to watch me as I pass through open doors
onto the lawn, into sunlight, between
peonies as between torches,
is for you to see me naked
as though you surprised a boy in private woods:
only the tips of my ears are covered
by my dark hair that captures close to you
the light in twisting rivers.
And my feet too are invisible, sunk
in seasons of needles and leaves.

And in your thought we are still there together
much later when, the lights lit and the screens closed,
I sit at the piano. You would say you are alone with me,
despite the others, and the notes
of Liszt and of Alkan, warmth chased with cold,
fall and dust across us. First you hear them
above, striking the leaves like light fingers,
and then at last they reach down, refreshing us,
releasing the savors from plants and from the earth.

A Natural History of Words

I almost recall the origin of these words;
on a night like the interior of coal,
landscape of shadows, although no light existed
to make it possible, no objects to cast it forth.
There was a pond with a dark internal fire,
a half-moon in the polished sky.
And a rim of low hills with above them
identical dark clouds that swelled
from their own inverted ground. It was a mirror
gazing in a mirror, and the one faulty symmetry
a being pierced by unmeaning whispers,
flooded with echoes.
Crying reflections: they plundered
a rib from lonely contentment, the old days
of silence and the sun
thrust into the quiet eye
on the blade of a pine needle:
a child's silence, all comfort and wildness

where at noon seeds and withered hands
and pyramids fell without sound
in the shadow of offices.

Then the dead returned but not in their own forms,
fire and cold which kill men became a man.
Never again would I fail to speak
to the many leveled city of bees,
or fear to trust my boat
to the ocean dissolved in evening.
Sometimes, between two woods shrinking in mist,
the whole earth seems to appear
in an almond of light,
suspending itself just above the ground,
from its fingers spreading the roads of the visible.

In all flesh, all mineral, all haze
and the most perfect clearness
there is speaking: conversations remembered.
But of the words, the speakers, what they said,
nothing remains, only a tone,
a shape to be filled with what occurs to us:
perhaps sadness, pride, desire,
love with resignation or triumph:
something that mingles with matter
and moves freely at the core.
The birds draw it out in their beaks,
it's the filament with which they link
the trees and the open spaces, afternoon and dusk;
it's the new path they invent
through this ancient park to which each second
restores a wilderness
greater than maze or mystery: a pleasure
planted here long ago
so there could be no end to understanding.

Desperate and Silent

And here before twilight was the bee,
desperate and silent, the phlox already
fallen in the high grass and shriveled
like drying droplets: milk and wine.
And again within the faint nervousness
of leaves, still fainter syllables

suffer against the ear, drawn out
to eternal shapelessness. In the soft
wall of evening, doors are lost
and behind them children bearing wounds:
of hunger or of heavy abundances,
of a vast face bending nearer, the coin
of night or the bullet of dawn.
And in the house behind, no source
of the soft crying that spreads out
is found in all the rooms passed through
hurriedly, left open-doored and lighted.
And no sound from the silver glass
standing on the dark table in the lawn
with faint light on it from the fireflies:
glass from whose bottom at each emptying
glows the shadow of a parted mouth.

Aftermath

We learned afterwards that defeat
introduces the mind to a new world
that is yet the old world, older
than we ever guessed, the world we knew
but with only one life in ten left living,
the gesture bereft like a brown fern
waving in light wind of the power
to change our course, the colors robbed
of power to sicken and revive.
It is as if the body becomes
a bottle dimming with the dirt of age
and into it we are repoured,
we who first poured ourselves out
as a medicine to nature:
and the yellow paleness of the place
is ourselves, grime on the stuck windows.

It's so long now, I can't imagine
what you may have become, what powers
have arisen in you, newly seeking
to soften the lesson of cracked clay
by floral disguise, what tears
may streak the dust with marks that seem
like more than human words. So much

that made the future clear
by its sympathy is left behind,
and looking back for it, my memory
withers, all promises once given
grow illegible. What comes back to me
is a story you told of an old man
you had known well, who nearly died;
and when you saw him later, walking,
he was powerless to notice you,
though you spoke to him and touched him:
confusion or fear had turned
his eyes and ears so inward.

LIGHT OF FLESH

Out of you
this gesture, a light of flesh,
radiates into air,
disperses in emptiness and becomes it.
It enters the invisible mouth
always open
to effort's fire and smoke
or to a motion such as this,
love's most casual breath.

It has gone, I want to say,
into memory, into comprehension.
But when I look for all
I was given of you,
where is it?
Although I swore to keep it
as I now swear to keep
this gesture
that flashed toward me
across a table.

I am vanishing down your eyes
as you sink into mine
and into air, wood, shadow,
into memory and comprehension,
all openings
that pour us into earth.
Justice has power in the mind

but your dying, a current
of senseless punishment,
carries everything away.
Whatever endures
must endure this.

BLUE LIPS

From this small rise at its center
the furrowed valley softly
radiates downward from your feet,
as gently curves up again
to ringing mountains:
a bronze cup growing green.

Above you there is the usual clouded weather,
the sky littered with undecided forms,
disturbed, pregnant with their own futures,
all moving in one direction
although it is not yesterday's.

And you are this scene,
the clouds, the sky and valley,
though within it you are only
the small, immaterial effigy
which lies in the center.
From far above, you see that figure
longing to be part of all it sees.

You almost taste that longing:
blood, which fills the standing cup
always clamoring beneath
your blue lips.

WHEN YOUR VOICES GO

When your voices go,
the sky's face with its smile
becomes a coincidence of cloud again.
Did we ever hear you? The sound we remember
was so much like the tide going out...
Now there is no one to suggest:

"Doesn't that branch
remind you of a man raising his fist?"
We wonder that this spot in the stone
once seemed the imprint of a hand.

And now to speak even a little,
like this, of loss,
she and I strain to the farthest border
and call out
to the point where your last trace faded.
Nothing has any effect now,
nothing causes another thing.
Sometimes we are rock, and sometimes
the rock ceases, we become
a huge space, a commotion in air,
a dissolution of tinted vapors.
But light with its power
to make things stand apart
is another dream. We rise
again into the dark block.

In these sounds, our voice,
is there repeated the presence
of someone like the one who left,
though "No one touches us"
is all they say?
She and I are singing forever
like wind on
a stone beside the river.
We are going through all the changes
of light in this small place,
bound on the way you called
"between the root and the flower."

A Secret

Echoes masked in return
had invented strange uses
for our voice. Our human
crying once—relative
to the bound flights of leaves
in rooms of snow and wheat—
heard them break the promise we called

to ruins, bright auburn, waiting
in the sundown to be repossessed.
Now each of us hides the same gift
from all the others: a vacant branch
that quivers, mourns for hints,
for touches from the air's
heroic fingers. Alone, we shake it
and unrhythmically morning's gold
moisture drips into the darkened
pool, onto colorless topaz,
lighted space, altar where the visible
waits to be offered. And only you,
earth, preserved us (you, the ancient
origin of errors and seductions)
from those reverberations coming back
out of misshapen hives on your hills
where our words became betrayers.
And still you keep us from
the half-people,
one-footed and one-eyed,
hiding in new deserts, working
ashamed, hating idleness,
who manufacture this disguise
for our voice, for your face...
your face splintered into levers,
and your intelligence, where now
we are a rumor of water,
a secret, the object
of priests and suicide,
a possession of sleep.

Permanence of Evening

As I walked down the Rue Placide, Maria,
your half-made bed flew beside me
at the level of the third floor windows,
the milky inside of your left arm like the story
of a stupid romance and a botched suicide.

Until at the corner of the Piltdown Road
it collided with Luce-Elaine, that pillar
of smoky gardens; she always comes
to this corner to meet and guide me.

And the two of you fell together with the sound
of piles driven at another building start.
There is so much construction going on, the city
changes from one week to the next:
if I were blind I don't know how I would live here.

Thus all my former wives combine themselves
into daughters to be my brides, my brides
stand around like towers tacked through the joints
of a giant butterfly spread out on the ground.

The result of my laudable attempts
to "deal boldly with substantial things:"
the river is never the same, but then
it is never any different, and all I want
is to be awakened every moment by dawn
in a place no one's ever seen.

TRAVELING

Since we last felt the need to travel
frescoes have intervened
that endure for centuries
dripping slowly from wet walls:
polished wings and breasts
up where it hurts the neck to look.
Congresses are held in that light
and the opinions of leaves have equal weight
with those of the potbellied prelate, the lamb
and the young girl in yellow organdy.
And it is impossible to guess the functions
of all those worthies
walking where olive trees and myrtles
are planted in the surf of cloud.
Nor have women been absent,
weeping by the stream with knives
they draw slowly down the skin between the breasts
like a zipper, revealing the beauty of man's body,
the black knives
which are a condensation of all space
into a useful implement,
a letter opener, the women's hands
which are a condensation of time.

All this has intervened,
held in the air of a hidden flute
under the beech trees, as still
as bees working in the clover at noon.

THE OWL

Good luck that summer, dodging among the clouds,
followed me like some owl that for my sake
had forsaken the wet dark evenings. From his wings,
the feathers snowed down on everyone I knew.
Loving women, good money, and plentiful ease
touched my friends as I passed, and their talents
dipped a toe in the gold that runs
in the air's veins. My brother
was taken up by the specter of my luck
and lifted across the Pacific to Japan
to bring the emperors knowledge of the piano
and of machines that lighten burdens and carry learning
beyond the sea. Everywhere in strange and happy mixture
I seemed to hear the notes of Beethoven
proceeding gaily and solemnly above the heads
of the feudal lords down the lanes of cryptomeria
to the Toshogu Shrine. The very clouds
where good luck hid itself were now
the exhalations of tea drunk to my brother.
I recognized them when they rolled over the mountains
to stir with their blazing sticks the stone
city of Guadalajara in its tall cup.
I saw the ancient alphabet in its sky,
and found a parchment there more full of water
than the plumpest reed, which bleeding as I wrote
began to wash false slogans from the walls.
What can I say of huge marriages beginning
in the smallest rooms, of flowers coaxed by my wife
from the deep shade,
happy sheep ripe for slaughter,
a dead voice crying from forty years ago,
freshening the western light with death?
I seemed to be on some liner on a calm ocean
far from any land, and this owl where no owl could be
lit on the bridge, right up where the sun is blinding.
Then I sat in a cemetery on the steps

of a large tomb, an imitation temple
with a padlock on its door against vandals,
the trees interpreting the late sun for me,
adding moist green and black, the owl
hidden somewhere among them. I thought how its feathers fell
and it seemed to me they were snow, that winter had come.
In the neighborhood all the roofs were covered with snow,
the streets were filled, the drifts came up to the sills,
and the snow gleamed, crossed with bony shadows
in the moonlight and the soft yellow lamplight
from the bedroom windows, huge like descending stars.
Even there, at rest in my tree, was the white owl.

REEDS

The two burning gears of the shades
roll in the machine that consumes itself
with sauces drawn from the wars.
It was before and after so much blood,
in those days when a brown man
was turned lovingly and slowly on a spit
and his color defended him
for centuries from migratory birds,
the anger of the leaves in passages.
Arrow in the sky, your point gathered
my viscera, tied in the peritoneum
and slung from your beak like a hobo's pack:
I saw you beaten in bronze
on your way to a copper fire.
So long ago, when the wind released
the scent of paper and ink from the willow's veil
on late afternoons when the sun in its dying
set forth across the Indian Sea.
I was there, I lived in a blueprint
with the nothingness of all those who would
inhabit the house: graphite,
the flies in the grass, and the two crossed beams
set up to cast a red shadow, to induce
some darkness of which night is a semblance,
and which lurks in the singing reeds to come forth sweetly
only when they have been beaten,
beaten to death.

On the Preserved Body of an Inca Child Frozen to Death as a Sacrifice to the Sun

The priests collected your teeth,
all your cut hairs from the ground,
the parings of your nails,
so that, dead, in another world
you do not have to go searching far
for the parts of your body.
And will you there be able to make again
from these immature scraps,
and from your frozen shell,
the head that shaded, mouth that spoke to,
hands that played with this silver
doll of the goddess, these flocks
of small gold cattle? If elsewhere
your strong fingers assemble the pieces
or if here the empty form
of your body, more real than the ice
that for centuries treasured up its flesh,
walks through us, still the sun's light
which makes us its instruments
can't find you. The sun
for whom you were staked in the snow
only fills the places empty of you,
making us see what is done
in his own false name
to the poor tongues of his fire.

Only Deeper

The brass mountains fell apart
and bridges cried, deposed
in the empty grammar
among statues' painted eyes,
pieces lying
between plaster fingers,
in the crooks of knees. That
is our wisdom: nothing
must be, the organs
are seized with an idea or mood,
transcend the body and destroy it,
and every bone with its thin

layer of dust prepares
its widowhood:
for the loved ones who just left
so naturally as if on a brief
outing will never return.
Already they are lying
spilled in the road, their simplest
lantern or sandwich
an ancient mystery now
to us, who find the remains.
Was it these who, living,
created and handed down
all we know, bequeathed us
anxiety before the dead
silence, before the stare,
the sleep, the acquiescence,
the ill will and peace
of ruined objects that once
made perfect sense
to hands now stiff
and eyes that have surrendered
to the light? And when at last
we have reconstructed the whole site
as it must have been,
still nothing speaks. Were these
the first to take the wrong turning,
so that every later route
only strikes deeper
into the same sad country?

IF THE MAN

If the man who is only eyes
and these eyes always open
frightens you, don't think of him
or of what he sees in the wind
that is a stirring of the encasing
stone. Instead
think of the man who is ears
that are palms of hands
that are the leaves of a forest
that is one tree.
He hears what he thinks he hears

and it flutters in his convolutions,
which lead from heart to heart,
hearts that guard the privacy
of people living in their chambers,
each alone. His sounds
bear them the messages
of absent lovers. He hears
everything without ceasing,
without rest: if this
confuses you, think instead
of yourself, of what you are,
wandering in the landscape
of these friends, these angels. Eyes
that are globes not cast in shells
and three-quarters darkened, ears
opened outward, not curled like rinds,
a body that does not turn
its back on the south to greet
the north, that faces both fire
and water, that drinks its fill
of both where the two are one
in a cup of blue earthenware.

Foundation

In the empty city,
a parade of identical stones
levitating along the sidewalks.

To the applause of brown hands
driven into heaps by the wind,
some old men remain, in the stadium
drinking cold coffee
from curved silent horns.

A word that no one would admit to his ear
rolls into the sewer
where green lights repeat prayers,
still unanswered, to themselves.

And a virgin weeps by the stream,
but she draws her hair aside
and she has no head,

she is only a skinny shaft,
a mop stuck in the mud,
singing to its image.

There used to be some tramps here
who dragged themselves past these crooked boards,
empty windows,
signs erased by rain.
On cold nights they burnt the shutters
and floors of decrepit buildings.
All that's left now is the dragonfly
startled from the stream bank
this cloudy October.
Noon is a kind of dusk.

All is shoddy, repetitious, evocative.
Everything engenders
the same fierce longing to be elsewhere,
perhaps at the bottom of the sea,
where lost wonders transform
a similarly murky and viscous frustration.

But in fact this is the bottom of the sea:
Atlantis, where wisdom drowned,
nation from which the flood never recedes,
where astronomers
watch Noah's keel high overhead
touch and moor to the mountain peak,
and the dark hulls of other lighted dreams
maneuver among pillars and arches
of white stone in the sky.
To this place the magi are always coming.

A city of hints, of something
ever more about to be,
of gestures the currents bend aside.
Here an inscription says: "If only
we could destroy the body." And another
answers it: "God is within
each thing. Do not insult with fasting
the potato, the dead flesh,
which have absolute command over the stars."

Winter Garden

All winter I have leaned here,
with snow coating my shoulders,
on this stick I cut in summer
to support me. It stabs
the cracking leaves: brittle webs,
fallen hands. I command
this stick, and this tree
whose branch it was, to blossom,
and in the motionlessness
that presses, in silence, I lean.

Inside the house a yellow light
fills up the rooms, fresh fruit
fills the bowls on the tables.
Here, snow and a black tree.
In this time of sticks,
of tarnished gold
lying confused with charcoal
among stripped stalks, the house
hardens itself, unshielded
by any green. Always it awakens
to overcast, the absence
above it of any source of power
for its rooms so full of wine,
burning themselves now
for some color, some motion.

And the dull places around me
under the hedges insist and call.
But silence and bodily misery
have rooted me; deprivation
and long listening feed my veins,
until I am a thing more eventual
than winter dusk. Here I will lean,
tottering, ever further decayed,
to see the day when the light
of those windows will detach itself
and rise. Then I'll feel again
a liquid coursing
in this torn branch. And the strange
spring that returns will be in my power
and submit to be known for my sign.

Jamaica

In Jamaica the soft rain at night
alternates with invisible blue stone.
Cats and women are lured into history
and falling limbs
band together in the pit.

Deposed rulers live there
because the rents are low.
They carry four grapes in each hand,
in the gaps between the fingers.
There is neon and the sound of dancing.

Lost among dark drapes and wet thighs,
frightened at first, a small girl
remembers this place is forest
and lies down to sleep. Morning,
and she is at her window again.

And under the skin the moving
tumor struggles and grows.
Explosion blue at night,
orange against the white and green of day.
Blue lips beneath the bright signs.

Rosy dawn throws its cross over the sea;
pyramids and spheres,
one form inscribed in the other,
the outer inscribed again
in a larger type of that which it encloses,

the idiotic symbols
filled with Jamaica's light: breasts
of a soiled woman in her shattered doorway,
the sweating pitcher of bloody marys
and its red ring.

And we seem to see the birds
whose names we don't know
impaled on Jamaican spears,
which also have unknown names
and which no one lifts anymore.

For banner, a dead bird lifted up
on shafts of light. Singing, an organ bird.
Dripping, a rainbow.
The carbuncles burst in the temples
and there are diamonds risen from the bone.

Asleep on Jamaica's fingertips
or whispering on the porch of its ear,
we feel the tremors of its service
awakening, as if a table awakened.
Light from the dark surface. A red word.

AT THE TOMB OF ANDRÉ BRETON

This is the grave,
the mouth whose tongue
sounds the anchoring note. If here
a large hand buried finds itself
touched by a small hand, the two
stay with this grave though soon
they go away together. Elsewhere
they lift their food to hollow mouths,
turn to each other and then turn back again
in pain. Here they will never end
becoming the human thing the air
has waited for so long
to feed from its grateful veins.
Here the breeching of light begins,
infant shadow engendered between
a blind being on earth
and this grave.

EAGLES

In the plaza the architects are gluing matches together,
matches whose phosphorus is so wet
that when they are struck by the sun
a flame that is visible but not felt
draws a veil of water across the windows.
A lifeless water, the color of algae:
a reminiscence of life
like the vibration of blunt fingers in October.

And now in the gallery of family portraits,
stations on a painful way, a frog
hangs yellow tiles on a skeleton.

The creation of the body: slim cathedral
bathed in dripping fats.
Here soon the worshipers will come
with their long nails
to etch their design over the figured floor.
The blood of their tattered fingers
will flow in the scratched furrows.
And in red fading to a lightless brown
the outline of an eagle appears,
abstract and eyeless, covering
the sexual eagle of god.

Poem for Gilberto Meza

I

Spring in the north. This is the hour
of the signs of hope: green bells
whose faint opening peal
softens the air; the blue sky
laying down its invisible sword
and coming close. It may be always
I feel this power in me,
but I only see its face clearly
for a while when it first drops
the mask of winter—mask
I have long planned to misplace
forever under a heap of years
to be thrown away. This is the hour
of a certain natural ease returning
to the homeless, the drunk, the ill,
a promise bitter because
it does not fulfill itself.
Yet the sting is dulled, for this pageant
of return has already passed so many times
and left nothing for those whose lost one
does not return; till now,
even the idea of such a blessing
seems to shame us, and the mask
of winter is lifted again.

2

Your Guadalajara is always raised
in a cupped brown palm and over it
a cupped blue palm is folded,
as if a careful girl were bringing
an injured bird
to her father. The city's waterfalls
of purple and glossy green
flow without falling
on its walls unfortified against any season.
Even the tourists hang
like sprawling flowers from balconies
or under fountains on the boulevards.
Yet children beg, dogs
battle to nourish their cancers,
and the Indian is mute
in the sun's glare on the mosaics,
in the shadow of the façades
carried from ancient Spain, near the arch
under the stairway
where Orozco's love is screaming.
Old men whose skins are sections
of the cracked, whitened soil
board buses, deformed
under the weight of fruit
gathered from the groves of the swimming club.
The factions plant shells
behind walls, and rifles and grenades
are ready to bloom at any season
in the hands of soldiers: strange spring,
held at ready by a power opposed
to the conspiracy of the elements
and man. In your city, too,
the inherited mark manifests itself,
the progress of living into dying
that seems to spread out to all things
from a source in our self-hatred,
and colors even the original, unflawed diamond
of your weather, which always smiles
but sometimes, briefly, will cry.

The Peasant's Soil

It is as though I cannot see this land,
as I cannot see my father's head, though still
I feel him walking somewhere nearby,
poking his stick among the ferns, greeting
every child and dog. Is this land, then, also dead,
and are these hills only its presence to me,
some ghost of itself, beckoning
with its ghostly scents, its air
I can never breathe deeply enough, into the dark,
open space I seem to hold
somewhere down in me, and beneath me?
Certainly the light is a ghost, which no hand
and no word ever touches,
and the sky is a ghost which nothing can embrace.

I talk, but in this land my words are only
a small figure almost eaten by day's brightness,
almost dazzled out of existence
on a bare hill or at the end
of a rutted road frozen by the sun.
We are unreal in each other, I and this land.
For in what I say, this land appears
faintly, at the edges, under the feet of my words,
as in a sketch where the man is so detailed
he is ready to live, but the earth and sky
are only a bare stroke or two, to remind us.
How much must be beneath us and beyond
if we want to live. And the intricate
work of lines, the man in the sketch, searches
for a soil within, behind, the gray ink wash
someone has spread to indicate the world.

I look at this land where I grew old,
and sitting before my door, I think
I have never touched it,
though I have ground its soil into me
and burned in its light till it remade
the color, the shape, the texture of my flesh.
It seems nothing could be more real than this,
which I have scarred and which scarred me in return,
which took and took from me
until I learned to yield to it what I wanted:

the short generations of grasses and animals,
my one generation of men.
And yet, if this land were here, they would be here,
and sometimes I understand the scent of the bean fields
at my elbow has come a long way, from overseas,
and has grown faint in the wind. Then more than ever
do the crickets, the flicker of the trees, the smell
of wet clover and hay become at once
mere shadows at my feet and something fuller
than the sun on any vine leaf: this land,
touched by an old man lost in what is lost.

THE DEATH OF FRANCISCO FRANCO

This is the bench where I wrote
the "Portrait of Francisco Franco." October 1975.
As Franco lay dying, clutching for death,
the impassive scientists in their unfelt fear
at this ending, gulf or bridge, trameled him
in wires and tubes and held him back.
Franco. I showed him: man playing tennis
with a lice-ridden chicken for a ball.
I described how his nose was a gun
which he blew in the petals of his daughter.
And I prayed for his dying to last long.
In the tipping autumn this stone bench was cold
and the veering winds shook me.
How watery was the light, streaked
with palest yellow and blue, while the colors
of the bruise and of the wound mounted
in the struck trees. Tossing light:
an agitated water. Light shaken
when the wind would twist and release
the decimated branches. And the curled shreds,
the dispossessed, the leaves, were still supple
with an imitation life, the last of sap
caught in the cut off veins. Lifted
from the ground or torn from boughs,
they eddied past me and dived in crowds,
shades of myth whirled by a last passion.

And the water in the sodden ground that seemed
to be rising in those rainless days

from a source in the earth—this moisture
was one with a moisture under my breast.
Some adolescent sadness had returned, a rising
of rain-fed waters. That noon of Franco's dying
echoed with a deserted evening that I felt
beneath my throat: a silent lake
devoid even of birds and singing insects.
Over it the sun is setting, and to its surface
rise patches of inflamed red and brownish purple,
as in the aftermath of a heavy blow.

  But the frenzy all around, and within me
the stillness burning silently,
a spark in ash—
all this energy and agitation among ruins
seemed the commotion of a spring
rising in October in spite of reason
and the year's cycle. A human spring,
escaping only when deprivation
has stripped the husk away,
when there is nothing left of its old world
for the seed to eat. Touching the external,
the soil, the water and the air, and feeling
above it through the mass the presence,
the possibility of light, it can begin at last
to augment itself and to live indeed.

  So we look forward to winter. Prisoners
deprived of the world, we will march alone
surrounded by rifles, bootless in the snow,
with only some old rags tied over our feet,
or nothing. Life is locked up in ice around us,
all is veiled, all is chained, and many die.
But we walk on, happy for the blinding edge
where white and blue fit together;
and happy for the crumb that falls
into our vast hunger like one drop of rain,
a drop that is a seed self-watered. A seed
falls in the desert: seed of rivers and lakes,
of hushed voices in the air, of gentle darkness
that colonizes the brooding day, pays itself out
in dances and arabesques: shade of the troubled leaves
reincarnating a harsh ghost of light.
Perhaps nothing we knew will ever come again,

it is all destroyed, and these images...
nostalgia, this sound of water
that bubbles in the openings of our senses.
There is no water anymore,
this is not desert, the new man
is not a man, and has no body. Here there is only
loss, pain, and very seldom an ancient satisfaction
felt by one man, the only man,
on a blank background—
nothing, abstraction, the end of the physical world.
Yet here a promise touches that which was.
Here we know nothing, we touch some object beyond us,
or person it may be: someone else.
And in the total dark, total light, in the absence now
of all the soldiers, of snow, the locked earth, the heavens,
what is it that reminds us of a child
destroyed before it existed, child that we were.

   That November Franco passed from death to death.
In life he was dust, and only the spit
of all good people
gave him weight and kept him on the earth,
stayed him in the real, prevented the wind
from carrying him off to the realm of pure cruelty.
In life he never awakened, but his snoring shadow
spread out over the world. There in Spain
they were covered by his anus and genitals:
an elephant hidden by a dime.
Here in America we were his left hand.
In his joints, conceived in arthritis,
cities and forests burned. How fat he was
in his polka-dot suit and tasseled hat,
surrounded by buck-toothed bald men even fatter:
so fat their legs could not reach the ground
and they rolled after him, grinning and picking up
the articles he kept dropping: dirty underclothes,
rusty popguns, eyeballs and mangled coins.
And sometimes when he led them down a slope,
unable to stop they rolled over him,
crushing him into the mud and hurtling
to the bottom, colliding, rebounding,
gently settling into a drunken heap.

But was it his shadow over everything?
Or did his body become the world, in which men lived in caves,
eating acorns as in the golden age,
sleeping by their clubs, hating and desiring gold
that lit the domes of Franco's south,
founding the faith of perfect opposition?
For what were they to do, hidden on the hillsides
with ancient rifles, seeing day by day
the glittering patrols pass in steep valleys below?
Nothing but rock all around, bitter weeds
and a stunted cork tree, its sparse leaves blown
like the hair of an ancient, balding woman.
Crouching not to strike their heads on a sky
hard and bleached with the cold, they felt
neighbors of that unearthly point
where the wind was created, where some bitter spirit
flees downward from the world's crown
seeking the warm sound of palms, and a body
patient, inert, on a hilltop, late afternoon.
The wind seemed to them their desire. They were close
to some desire that was pure where all was cold,
bare, nearly invisible: a desire
that had scarcely any body
and yearned toward the south where Franco
tricked out his corpulence in fat commanders,
miters, museums, women, the year of fashion,
the gestures of stone and oil. Desire
without a body: what can a ghost do
but howl and beat itself
against the wall of flesh, its tiny buffets
with no more power upon substance
than the tides of a reflecting pond
where the sun lies among long blades?
"Must the whole universe fall into ruin
before we can destroy this man?"

There on the porch of winter Franco died
and the leaves were driven around my ears
by a violence like spring's: strengthless shapes
carried past on the self-contradicting air,
savagely excited, starting in passion
and in passion turning back upon itself;
so clear that everything entered it, passed through it,
and it blew violently on all,

detaching fragments, bending, breaking,
furious and strengthless, destroying that which falls.
As if the bonds of slavery that hold
the beautiful surfaces together, the bodies
which create love, were broken and all the parts
were loosed onto currents, into confusion.
All that we hated, all that we opposed
is broken up. A winter-in-summer is ended,
summer of seductive ice, the fleshly glow
shining among reeds and green mounds,
and over the face of the strictest wall
a soft wind and birds in the blue-flowered vine.
O sack of corruptions: body that we loved,
falling apart, as a rotten mass in autumn
goes its separate ways on the stream,
or as ice shatters in spring.

   In what false season did Franco seize
everything we had made and seem to take it
body and soul into his intestine? He drove you
far from Spain, your body, body of dreams,
Joan Miró, Benjamin Péret, Jorge Guillén;
and he drove many friends still farther,
till they were only shadows and words in light.
Then the cathedrals spit out jackals with whom
there is no argument, and from opened books,
from before the men and landscapes stretched to breaking
of El Greco, rose thick ghosts who stuttered and laughed,
leaving no room for men in Spain. Men fled
to dark corners, forgotten basements, wild hills:
the whole world to them became a cave
where no fire was lit by night, while the enemy
possessed the fields full of vines, the factories,
the day's light that draws redeeming colors
even from rubbish, and makes the least thing
strong. But did anything that these men said,
anything that I said, sitting here on this bench
in October 1975, persuade those hands
that reached at last through nature and bit by bit
tore Franco into death? Only our living,
which is the aging of the world, and was Franco's aging,
had that power. It released those winds
of late autumn, tugging at the last leaves,
the last scraps of flesh on the skeleton,

and today again those winds are loose,
the masts and rigging of the earth bared,
and the hulk rolls, the clouds that reveal
light continents are closing together, all color
begins to resign itself to a steel-gray.
But let the hardness and the pain that comes
be a scalpel. Let the sharp edge
of blue wind on snow-encrusted field
cut Franco's rotting hands from the legacy.

  It is the time when everything seems husk.
The love of one way, one summer though it betrayed,
asks hate for the hard season that approaches.
But winter light is the wildest, the calmest,
holding the most of ruin and exile
in the simplest look. And when the cold
has locked up all around us, we sit apart
in houses or walk in the false fading tropic
within our clothes, like a man in empty space.
We are cut off, gone out of things,
and we think our own thoughts,
free among the uncivilized powers,
examining a splendor, loose in a beauty
before all kindliness. That which we are
does not always upholster itself in comfort
or even life. And now the mind
falls crazily away from all it sees
and yet is rooted here, unmoving, pure
as the sky of this moment, incapable of change.
This falling which is buoyed up, this sureness
of death attended with the knowledge
that it can never come: this too is a summer,
summer of human things, where Franco's fleshy hand
turns to nothing as it gropes to seize
a conception. Here, in winter,
things grow to be no more than the bone of themselves,
and we will fall farther, to where the bone
and the bone's dust have never been: beyond,
exiled, outside of everything,
to the pith of earth's next summer
when the forms are given back,
when that which is meant is said.
The feathery leaves come out in the street
and among them the lamps light

of their own accord. And men return
to monuments that begin to move,
to a deserted city intact, to empty land
already staked out in farms, where Franco
is a dried leaf that blows away.

The Visitation

I   Music and Exile

What They Prayed For

What they prayed for seemed not much,
and already, despite the dusty weeds
extending to the sky, a possession:
a grassy land, lightly wooded,
rolling, with intricate slopes
and crossed by streams, relieved
by lakes, pools and reedy swamps.
Breezes over the water to suggest
music; and, visible from rises,
the ocean, glinting among the trees,
near so that when you are silent
within yourself it can be heard.
Also shade and shadow:
an openness to the sun,
to the sky, that is yet defended
and moistened by fingers of the earth.
Then a few things will follow
from these first conditions: women
singing in full light and at dusk
before reflecting water;
and some way to live together
that is not a scandal and a shame.

Signs and Certainties

Look for the time when in the woods
the walnut tree will dress herself
in the fashion of flowers
and perfume her head and neck;
if her fruit overwhelms you
with the sight and the thought of it,
later in the year the grain too
will be overwhelming
and the overburdened threshing
come in an abundant heat.
But if poor in fruit
she spreads herself into leaves
and covers the ground with shadows deeper

than black water, then the straw—
nothing but chaff—will be pounded
on the floor with no result.
And I have seen the farmer's pods,
though bred long and with great care,
still fall and rot on the ground
unless year after year the man
picks off the largest. So everything
falls backward, runs from much to less,
as a rower in a strong river,
if he relaxes for a moment,
is swept down toward the sea.

THE CROW

Here all analogies
conflict, waver
and run together. The sun
is the eye of heaven.
But earth too is an eye
connected by a long cone,
a nerve of shadow,
to the black fluid behind.
All day it closes
its blue lid
and someone comes
to batter the calm mask
with his look
that shines through,
burning down on the secrets
of the sleeper.
The white spot moves
as he moves from left to right,
watching. His brightness
forcing through tiny veins
raises the quiet
swollen corpses that float up
and shine,
raises and separates
the glinting dark
lacework of trees.

What is the crow that lifts
from their shattered crowns,
where the light drips,
and arcs under the eyelid
across the eye?

Its cry echoes out,
a voice
of that stare burning into
this sleep.

Plunder

You see small clouds descending
to navigate among trees,
makeshift rafts of white branches
lashed together
with their foliage still living.
They float down the disturbed
currents of blue stone
foaming among these green islands
through deep or shallow channels
over dark caves. But you can't see
what traders pole them through the maze
with skins of unknown animals
from the tangled interior
of a continent of light—
a puzzled savage
watching as a wealth hidden from you
in your own heart
is delivered to another world.

On the Dial

Once ages ago the blade of a clock
for the first time circumnavigated the dial.
And now that frail ship repeats endlessly
its conquest, and men go aboard
to see again the ever-virgin blank.
There the furrows of predecessors close
without a seam yet all is already known,
the simple motif of a cross drawn in the water,

an x-axis and a y, is a perfect map.
Some, caught on the horn,
must eat their sails to live.
Many are mistaken for gods
and jealous priests stone them
on a speck of dust in the blue
hollow between two o'clock and three.

CHICORY

The staff the gray man carried
was a human spine: perhaps his own,
so shapeless he was,
his face an agèd web.
Why was he there in front of the dirty sky
billowing slowly, another smeared outline
some acid was digging in the cloud?
All March he vanished with the dwarf
Himalayas of the gutter, but left his staff
rooted in mud, swaying
under the wires. There it ascended,
a steep and broken stairwell
whose building had long decayed.
For weeks it hung its dusty flowers.
And then someone passing saw
the chicory twitch in the wind
and recognized his spine:
the twisted column
he had known in sleep. He felt
his posture assume its shape,
his hands and eyes to be those flowers,
blue scars of a vanished body
still burning through the air.

PIANOFORTE

In the beginning I was a dismembered thing.
Then I felt from east and west converge
the ivory, mahogany and brass,
the idea of my form.

For years I stood
in a room at the level of ripe apples
and listened to my voice.
For years I waited alone.

The house decayed and through centuries
I hung in the air between the wooded hills
watching invisible waves triumph as ghosts
in the stone village.

The river became a marsh and then the sea.
Never moving, I lived under the ocean,
inside a mountain, on a wooded plain.

There is neither justice nor mercy in the motionless scales.
In winter starving sparrows freeze on my strings.
Still for a sin against the forgotten dead
the snake, without feet or hands,
eats the dirt under my ladder of keys.

Capriccio of Roman Ruins

We, the living ones, are distinguishable
from those we move among, people of stone,
by the red and blue of our robes,
the blood-glow of face and arm.
We lounge on the worn steps beneath
the last arch of a shattered roof
where the vegetation hangs, and two of us
are arguing a point, gesturing
to the empty pure blue sky. Another, alone,
dangles his feet in a little pool of rain water,
leaning against a toppled frieze; and one walks,
very slowly, back and forth, before the breached
dome of a tomb. But in the frieze
those others, gray or white, in colorless
garments of rock, are lounging
on their elbows by a little pool.
Or on the surface of a huge urn, filled now
with accidental dust and vines,
those carved ones talk and circle slowly
through eroded façades and marble alleys.

And one of them, a naked giant,
leans idly as though to mock us
against a broken column already a ruin
long centuries ago, when he relaxed
and upright, with open eyes, here fell asleep.

Thoughts in a Bank Elevator

Vandalized parking lots and globes descending from the sky
to the accompaniment of music long turned to dust
in desks of the sixteenth century—so dusk fell
on the determination to write a saga.
The characters stood knee-deep in a sodden dawn,
wrapped in blankets, as the survivors of a hotel fire
stand in the street among the hoses and watch the torpid
steam go up. Hotels, night clubs, ships and bridges—
always in these focal points of disaster
an exemplary company gathers: the Jew, the gigolo,
the drunk and the ingénue, the nigger, the handsome man,
all ordained by some power to come together and fall.
The night man brings gin, the cards are riffled,
a bell rings, the darkness shifts, past the window
a lame horse drags rocks from a far-off quarry.

Meanwhile, hypnosis is a possible answer
and the winds assemble at the mouth of the Ganges.
Also, Loki remains at large, the bat gathers dust,
Nemo still sleeps beneath his island
and the new man, pure product of science and engineering,
careens over the Antarctic blocks. It all might be
a pool of vomit outside a bar, or ashes
floating down from a father's righteous will
discovered first and burnt by greedy cousins:
some particles expelled
from an idea of what might be.

Never Did I Let You Be Deceived

How did you vanish on the waterways
of my orange palm, leaving only
the smoke of your hair among the clouds?
Never did I let you be deceived

by the fatal glamor of understanding.
It was yours to feel the stars
like fish nibbling at the flesh
of a rotting lily sprawled on rust-colored streams.
There existed your history, your future
and no enlightenment: only the desolation
of small blue suns sucking at green veins
that struggled from the roadside.

Thus I encouraged you to dismiss the things
that are not real: the dusty masonry
of which the air is made, the darkness
that sprawls upon me now while you
count the sparkles in the sands of India.
India, where you are lost.
Blessèd India, palm of my hand
displaying its mortal wound.

ANOTHER DON JUAN

You are greeting a blue woman
and this morning you swore faith
to the green, the shadow-streaked.

There are no candle flames
of moisture now on every hair,
no chaos or paradise
of feathers.

Only a silence of clover flowers
before the wooden pier, the white boats.

Already, fainting from a kiss,
you expect her of the red hand,
the cold black space between the breasts.
A flight of crows will vanish
over the maple grove in damp air.

But they are all one.
Even she who comes after,
she whose orange hair is falling,
who hides under warm lids
her white marble eyes.

It's noon.
The shade of the walnut tree:
a reminiscence. And its ridged bark
remembers the worn face
of the fathers.

In spite of yourself, to earth
the vow is kept.

Letter Written from the Country to One Engaged in Charitable Work

Still after so long your image often comes,
making me take its part against the love
of luxury that holds me. Where are you now,
at this moment? Somehow I ceased to know you.
But still I can see you in some featureless hall
with doors open on cancers,
hearts failing before the minds are eclipsed.
And what is the purpose of this over-nice
care for words, which pleases very few?
Thinking of those for whom you carry water,
I was seized with a fear that has not left.
How am I well and aloof while they,
in pain, are subjects of this verse?
I can rise at will after a day spent in sleep:
some misfortune, surely, is about to descend.
There's a foreboding in these mild diseases
that require for their contraction, suffering and cure
only a leisure the unfortunate do not have.
The weeks are a hospital where, recovered,
someone is stretching out a convalescence
in restless reading of many books, writing of letters,
which ruins the eyes for out-of-doors.
I remember how I used to visit you,
stepping out of the car, ringing your bell.
To discuss these things alone, we would walk
in the public garden where there were clean shadows
and busy citizens on plazas dissolved by light.
Museums, churches that lined the narrow park,
even the college, were not tedious with you beside me.
In the evening, after dinner, I could touch your hand.

Music and Exile

You are the only tenant who never leaves
that hotel forgotten in the hills
that I love and visit at all seasons:
muddy spring, summer of drenched crops,
autumns and winters veiled in rain.
There some disease working from underground
has changed to purple the huge fleshy trees.
And there you come down the steps, wander the halls
among the political refugees
who live there briefly, always flowing through.
You never join them at the sleeted windows
where they stand looking out nervously
along the road, expecting the police.
In the evenings you weave through them in the bar
while they play chess and cards
and ceaselessly form governments in exile,
and it makes you smile faintly to hear
their harmless manifestoes.
Your thoughts turn to the women in rooms above
with children as white as worms,
young wives whose flesh quickly grows gray.
It's as if they are falling into dust
here while they linger in life
thinking of gardens around their parents' homes.
And in imagination, imagination alone,
you place a light hand on the children's heads
because they never play
and they look at you with the same knowledge
that visited your girlhood.
Yet they are even without your desperation,
your power to be drunk with defeat and memory.
You think of fires never built in the snow.

Some say that mine is a work of images
appearing and ceasing to exist in succession,
like static and silence on a radio tuned at night
to some station perhaps beyond its range:
there is only nothingness to connect the flashes.
How is it that no one has detected you,
your voice, the thread of all things seen and heard?
Is it that you are not an image
but a ghost, the idea of a melody,
a cry from beyond the loud wall of the rain?

The thunderstorm lights up this inn almost in ruins.
The sky is a huge man
whose blood is on fire.
All night, one after another, the sections
of his network of veins explode:
for a second we see the jagged paths
cut off at their ends
fading in cloud.
The storm casts an intermittent gleam
on the inn where the lights have flickered and gone out.
Now and then the lightning picks out the faces
in a glow of gold and thick red.
Sometimes a few words are exchanged in darkness.
One hopes to obtain false papers.
One plans again the murder
of the officer who tortured his wife to death:
but that was fifty years ago
on the edge of Asia,
and the officer must be dead in the war
or of some disease
or peacefully, covered with honors, among his children.
The chess game continues in the dark
in their huge memories distended by idleness,
and the flashes give time to make a move
that already they have meditated for ages:
always the same adversary,
the same losses and gains.

And you:
you know that there is nothing within their power,
not even the coils of rope and the pistols
that some have hidden in their rooms:
occasionally there is suicide
but another always comes and fills the place.
Now, oppressed by the storm passing swiftly over,
they are thinking of the locked borders,
of freedom in the mountains,
and they don't see you pacing in and out among them.
But I hear you, I hear the rustle of your dress
and I know you love me.
I wish I could awaken and find you with me.
Softly you are speaking to yourself, to me,
and now I can almost see you
where you sit unnoticed at a dirty table
in the darkness shuffling, reshuffling the tattered cards.

Fire

In orange light by the motionless river
relaxing, you invited me
to consider the evil precedent
of fire. "Fire," you said,
"destroys the body, turns it to ash
as though it were some residue of salvation
precipitating into hell.
If you have burnt a piece of bark,
then for a momentary warmth
and a light that floated off
where you won't follow until death,
you have had to watch a fair thing
blacken and curl." Your voice
winding out and disappearing
with its faint heat like silver smoke
into twilight was the greatest pleasure.
After that, its accompaniment: the crickets
and fireflies that varied night's
border with the day's last motions.

Fire Song

A shell has burst:
O fire a deeper auburn than your hair.
It burns among the graves.
The chisel and the spade are absent
and unseen birds inflate the trees on the slopes.

A tall flame descends from a limousine
to read the names of the dead.
Among spiked fragments of the shell,
the squirrels are eating devastation.
Will there be another child of wood?

You wait for the snow
and from it the evidence or gift.
Flakes of fire sift down
on the bastions of the stonecutter's art:
O fire a deeper red than your memory.

The Scented Path

Spring: again
I enter the scented path
and a hoarse shriek of alarm
explodes from the half-open beaks
of the tulip tree. The sumac
burns with a dripping fire.
Shining beetles
staggering in the air
barge against my shoulders.

A locomotive without cars
rattles through the valley.

And here above, within three birches,
is the fountain called "Good Will,"
which they clean desperately each year;

and at its center, your statue,
which in spring pours water
and every winter leaves
a new layer of dust and brittle
pieces in the basin.

Your statue:
an armless torso now
raised into the air
on two rusted iron poles;
to the left one
a white thigh still clings.

Another bitter season
and the only sound of water here
will be the rain.

A Pliant Hand

Here if the sky at dawn recalls
some ancient passage or flight
mounting its scale of adolescent color,

in the acrid perfume winding
between lindens over littered slopes,

this is legend:
so once it was to live
even between serried edges
and the spirals shaved from steel.

And if nothing now
condenses that day dispersed
in the bright flash of shapes
blown across plazas of the lexicon?
Still an evidence—a late spar
or a rotted branch—
is cast on the beds of kelp.

And rigged again by dissolving
fingers of salt and rain,
swiftly the drowned bark, its odor, bears
an hour across the roaring
of tides congealed.

It continues: where the locust trees
filter the inhuman
from sky and water, a pliant hand
explores the moss. And you clasp it—

how dead it is,
how absent on this earth.

Persephone

Do you maintain
your integrity down there in hell?
Beneath my foot crushing the grass,
the shuffling unlifted steps beheading flowers,
I feel you. The flame
explores your body, a liquid hand
that probes and molds itself
into all openings: eyes, lips,
and those bays through which you let the tides of the earth
and men wash into you, through which
you sent your sugary winds
out over the ceaseless unfolding of water and salt.
Have you found something to keep you—
a chastity that can guard itself

even in sleep and chains, to push away
the smoky eternal persistence of your husband?
I see him: and in the blue spaces
between the clouds, ashes begin to fall
to teach me this season is no spring.
What pain enrages him: his hideous youth
ever renewed; his curling hair
that hides and grows from his body
to lengths of world-encircling smoke;
or his ardor, that has no forging power,
but only involves all things
in this cold glow and softening heat?

In the Garden of Gethsemane

I am only an ear
engrafted to the earth
by a little dust mixed with blood.

An amphitheater, a spiral shell
where the voices of men once eddied.
I remember angry words,
the sound of air parted by a sword.

Then I lay among callused insteps
and hooklike toes that seized earth,
anchoring straining bodies.

They are gone, forgetting me.

I have heard bones creak and snap
and men cry out
but even these ghosts fade.

I am new, silent,
and I say within myself:
What, empty funnel,
can you feed the earth?

Perhaps the white notes that now
in grateful darkness
fall through the tongues of the olives.

The Prisoner

Beneath the moor hens battered with rain,
a prisoner abandoned by his prison
returns to a barn
where a wounded lantern is bleeding on the straw.
Pelted with ice, he flings the familiar door aside.
For a moment (it is midnight) the cows
are touched with intelligence and know the story:
there is an intricate dark palace beneath a bed;
the spaces between the stars sing,
and tongues wander among towers
windowless and filled with light;
behind a closed door in a throat,
still, a chord vibrates.

The throat: but it is an empty room
where endlessly before a window
a woman is ironing. She sees beyond her
blackbirds around a lake,
clinging sideways on the reeds,
and from their trills vast domes expand
and build the sky. The woman sees herself
go out and lie beside that lake.
And at once the whole enclosing country
is only the hollow within her breast.
She has not moved, gone outward;
it is all part of her—that lake
surrounded by reeds where blackbirds perch,
and where a soft white stone is parted
to admit a visitor who does not arrive.

The skin strains for a light kiss.
But it is granted only beyond a wall
the body does not scale; or not, at least,
in this poisonous rumor poured in its sleeping ear,
this envy of its weighted crown.
There comes a little whisper, a tatter of something vast,
a wing of burning fog: the lost dominion
attacks the head with the head's own poverty.
For a moment the door is thrown aside.
The hail stabs at the straw
and in the open doorway a key dwindles,

the lantern of someone going back through the windy dark.
The unwelcomed guest returns
beneath the moor hens battered with rain.

VIEWS

This huge tree: sleeping
against its trunk, we thought
the stars were its distant berries,
the sky its foliage, the sun and moon
a pair of mating birds
who wove a monotonous chase
of courtship through its limbs.
Sleeping, we thought the claw of its root
clutched the shreds of a torn
idea, gathered them in a ball
and made continents, gave form
to a grateful remnant of water
beating, bodiless fists,
at the walls of wall-lessness.

One coming upon our bodies
as we dreamed there
in spring found them green,
hard, bitter. In summer, returning,
found them too beautiful to touch,
at morning and evening
covered with cool, fresh tears.
In autumn they seemed to him soft,
brown with irresolution,
in the act of deciding like penitents
to give themselves back.
In winter he found nothing
but a hallucination of two lovers
in the snow in the zero weather
twining in a shell
of their own light, naked
and unbothered, cold as the cold,
like stars fallen on earth
in the spot where we had been.

Next spring, two small forms appeared
near our places, and while these
were not ourselves, to the watcher
it made small difference—he praised
some shadow of us and them.
So the air shook with fear,
or was it anger? Night
became unreal. We awoke.

Now, in the day, with what
care we treasure the dream.
Of that tree, we make our tongue.
The voiceless sky we call
our skull, and to night's silent thoughts,
frozen and distant, we give words.
We rest, enjoying the watcher
as we recall him, his puzzlement
and sadness at our slow passing,
his horror at the pure winter glare
of blessedness where we withdrew
and apparitions followed.
We love his speechless
pleasure at spring and the forms
which return, in which he loves us.
But we do not return.
All this we recall while outward
our eyes are opening
into a city of mere light.

II   AREAS

1 BADLANDS

Will a day come again
when my eyes cease to oppose
a deserted glare over the earth of copper?
The yellow grass in tufts
is reflected in yellow clouds:
my glass, where I see no face but another mirror.

Streams shift in withered hills
and skeletons are revealed, embedded
in sandstone: fossil embryos that roost
in my limbs made mineral.

A hammer is launched against my jaw.
What is my secret?
Give me a part again with beings
that move their hands and, thoughtful, speak.

2 City Park

Gray and still are the locked
branches, the leaves unmoved
by any autumn or wind:
so it is in the light of the lamps
human on their metal stems,
inert conduits to the flow
of current in the earth.

And where the globes are broken,
one exhumed root is blown over the grass
until it stretches out beneath a willow
and takes a new form: invisible
shadow of this tree
where the only light is a veiled star.

3 Lake Beach

By this remnant of a glacial sea
the locust trees irrigate the light,
aspens leaning from the sand
broadcast their seed
to search corroding shores.

And hands dangle where uncomplaining
grass comes to the water's verge,
or in the dunes uncover
the bony claw of last year,
already ancient.
So many forms of death are long
familiar to these margins,
do they tremble at another:
the volumes of heated water,
lead a new essence in the blood,
the ceiling of choking knots
that shadows the species?

Still the light goes up from gray
water to sky, as though a dwarf
were dreaming his proper form.

4 Creek Bank

Still among the sharp-leaved
water plants, occasional flowers
silence the overhang of brick.

Still at times in those aisles
of shade along the shallow river
almost closed by reeds,
vigilance is forgotten
except by things in burrows
or colored like the grass,
motionlessly watching a bold foot.

There, slipped from the screen an hour,
the human glance wanders again, careless,
along the veins of leaves.

5 Creek Bank in Early Fall

There was no bird or fish,
no breathing in the air,
and yet the stream and the space above it
under the high apse of branches
were living to the eye.
On the water passed
schools of red and yellow leaves,
maple and beech.
The dead leaves fell
between flashes of the sun
on sumac blades, on wet stones,
glinting and twisting more
than a war of birds.
White seeds, curled feathers
revealed the arabesque play of that air,
which to the immobility
of human flesh was still.

6 Creek Bank in Late Fall

Today you are almost fully awakened, O confused branches,
from the cunning dream by which you fooled yourselves,
loved and betrayed yourselves—the leaves.
The tattered outlines left are not enough
that memory can rebuild palace or crown.
These as the mind delves
crumble to finer dust, more darkly recede,
at last achieving the subtlety, the depth,
of never having been. The eye
wraps itself in the cataracts
or humid soil of its own seeing.

And if rivers full to the brim
still slowly slide by banks where the grass looks over,
a simple sound, always equal but always music,
inexhaustible, refreshing, new,

calms and oppresses the mind repeating without end
phrases even the maker cannot hear
with pleasure or assent.

7 Ravine

August: this slope, whitened, trembles
with struggle of downy seeds, wind shifted,
locked in stiffening half-broached pods or caught
in yellow grasses
under the twisted sumacs' blaze,
wild apple trees and shattered birches.

With fallen seeds, matted and compressed,
the steep path is slick. Some drift above,
at times a stronger gust will rip from the bank
unbroken streams that are hurled up and spread
far away, falling slowly
down on the tangled screen that masks the river.

And so might a power strike, driving some part of what is mine
to fall elsewhere, in distant earth...

8 Remnant of a Woods

Mute both in peace and fury
the aisles among my pillars
changing direction at each step,
baffling progress, as motionless
as summer and the action of heroes,

for years uninhabited I slept
beside you. At last you hollow
a space in me and the pure light comes through.
A space—where is my body?
Water burns in the air.

In me, noon was a shade. But now
brittle and sweating at its torrid mouth
I call for night—

only a fringe that rustles
at the edges of my earth.

9 Field at the Edge of Town in Early Spring

With anxiety it struggles
to this littered shore: the sun
on decimated clouds borne northward,
opposed by gray roads and veins.
And in the swamps it releases
congealed sounds, in the stubble
exhumes colors of a season
that seemed eternal once but now
labors to return.

And again the shattered form
that covered the field does gather
flesh of bright vapor and rise from the green pools.

10 Cavern

Within dense flesh of moisture-quarried
limestone it echoes:
voice that does not exist.
Not hunters dead among their paints
in a throat of rock; only dust
driven about in unseen corners
without water to lay it,
without seed.

Why, locked in the cells,
does it call from so deep down
to the surface—
mute dissonance loud within
this copse where tender larvae
make brittle lacework of the leaves?

11 Ocean Beach

Again the torched continent
of a day's cloud drifts off,
dropping the last light.
Enclosed in this charcoal air:
vultures on rotting weed,
sound of drums from the night clubs,
driftwood and broken glass.

But still in the light—like a noon
shrouded in smoke or dead water—
figures are made: the tiny crabs
at the feet of children playing late
draw their quick lines in the sand.

12 Fog Hollows in Town

Nothing gives sign that I have passed
with evening and the torn salutes
of frogs along the marshy creek bed
and the railroad bed emerging
from ditches muffled in algae.
No omen, not the cry by night

of a crow on telegraph wires,
hints that I watch
the fishermen around their lantern,
the woman working late
in the hum of an electric clock.

And it seems that time for me
has died, passing beyond its end:
slow river dispersed in marshes.

Yet in my surface placid
as though frozen, a nervousness
still stirs: at the last hour
of night a mist exhales
in the widening air.

III   PRAYER FOR PROPHECY

PRAYER FOR PROPHECY

May the old women of music, frozen
in days before memory into words
(they cooled and suffered into use
between anvil and hammer), give
my ear a rumor of why the stars
flee and in what directions. Not
how the atoms and the grids of force
assembled like network the inept
sprawling design, but the future,
for which the loose lip of the sea
drools on this beach, sucking down
the dissolving sand. To what
purpose each winter the moaning chords
of night drag out their limp tails
longer, and with reptilian stares
rekindle soot in the day's face.
And if to this depth of nature I
am not destined to reach, then let
the country and the streams of water
that freshen valleys content me, hiding
in their sluggish harmony the cold
springs of the blood that clogs my heart.

POVERTY

This perspective: a green fly at rest
upon cracked paint of the railing
against a screen of many textures mixed
by light wind: basswood, box elder,
chokecherry and maple leaves.

And then the evening: light adrift
without object in emptiness,
the dismembered spectrum, orange in the west,
tatters of gold and purple flaring above
intangible greens—like some headless body
that dreams and does not doubt
a future cry
reconvenes its members.

And here the eye: stricken
by each separation and each fusion,
each shower of blows
which in love falls on the earth.
The pupil is a thirsty well
where these things enter and, echoing, die.
Not even dust remains
in that reservoir, not even ghosts—
only some shadows cast there
by its own toppled mouth.

THANKSGIVING

Now that the baseball season diminishes,
the furry seal will come to bask on the tiles
before our onyx stove:
onyx and ebony with the spattered cumulus
of a turkey dancing in its pyrex pyre.

O bankroll! Now Mexico recedes,
Japan advances and still
we are only a fugitive rhythm.
Gaily we meditate around the bird
the doctrines of entropy and fate.
Mayhap even Bo Diddley is not eternal
and the evening star
wastes its light in the last blue.

Ask the missionaries of Charles Fourier
(they are ourselves)
for a word that saves. We aspire
to sleep and endless chess games in the tomb
with the strawberry maidens.
Is there some life in thus outstaring
the blind beach we would comb
forever—their sandy hair?

LOCKED CUPBOARD

The sun-weighted air is empty
of birds, clouds, and all but flies
humming close to the grass.
It is a noon for feeling
the air on naked skin.
But a road passes near,
one can smell the baking tar—
and sometimes, twice a day,
a car suddenly may appear
and vanish, blind windows glinting.
On the flat harrowed plain
the single file of trees
left standing
between the outbuildings and the fields
is depthless, cannot hide
even the palest, thinnest body.
Deep in the house
a heavy oak door is closed,
all is so still the dust ascends
and a boy pours white liquid
from a locked cupboard,
taking care to replace the key
exactly in its mark on the wood.

GYPSIES

The man opens his fist,
closes and opens it tirelessly
to see still another time
the half-dollar
a neighbor has put there.
The sun, too, is burning

in the creases of the sky.
False brick peels from a wooden house
and burnt carbon sifts down
on vegetables near the mill
where the wagons are drawn up.
From the ditches filled
with sunflower and tiger lily
comes the wail of a child
stolen and forced to see
the length of the roads.

WHO REMEMBERS

The sky endures in its unhappiness.
They said it was a brain that unravels above,
shot with white lights, rolling like smoke or steam
around blue bridges that erect themselves and dissolve
among shifting islands in the space
of an electrocution or an enlightenment.
They said, "This is no drama: where is the denouement?
This is today like yesterday, even if yesterday
was pure and now it is filthy poison or storm.
This is your confusion."

                        As the thunderhead draws up
and engraves itself in twilight over the isolation
of a late bee, the warm air embalms
this new rearrangement of the elements.
There is no end to what is possible.
Now, as the bee changes flowers in a spike of phlox,
crowds move in Asia, a shot leaps on the hills,
a girl with a blue eye and a brown eye
passes beneath a bridge.

                        And now all is changed.
But there is one who never changes, one
who remembers all that can never be remembered,
who calls to the possible, the unfolding,
to the griffin, the sphinx, all beings that might be,
and longs for the one that comprehends.
Again his head on this day like every other
falls forward in the grass. There in the future
a barren circle appears, where all that is possible
has come to an end, where salt was sown in the earth.

The Mantis

My goal was absolute memory—to be filled with everything bitter, but to be like an infinite ocean always clean.

And seeking things to cherish—losses, forgotten beings—I recalled the mantis that when children we found and kept in a bottle.

It was our god. We wanted it near us, perhaps to punish if it worked no signs.

Who knows how to care for a god? Did it eat the leaves we shredded, enjoy the air that circulated through pin holes?

Its gaze, so attentive in a head like a pyramid overturned. Its postures, so suddenly assumed and graceful. Its continual silent listening.

We wanted to befriend this thing that had walked over our hands as if they were twigs and stems.

All day the animals we saw seemed one family, belonging to the mantis. The raccoon, the muskrat, the catfish and hornet: his wife, son, brother- and sister-in-law.

Then we forgot, and a few mornings later found the mantis stiff in the jar. His limbs easily came away from his body.

The opened bottle gave off the stench that later we knew again in zoo logical laboratories—a by-product of exact knowledge.

This had been the mantis's only work, the most difficult to perform for immortals: to die.

To die to his life among the grasses, which my memory, still holding the mantis, has never known, cannot recall.

The Bushman in New York

1

"You that are rich, you have your consolation."
So, a graduate of the university, many miles from the hut of skins,
I recall a few words from St. Luke as they were taught me at the
        mission school
where I first learned of clothing and practical mathematics.
An engineer now, I gaze back at my reflection
in the polished toenail of a giant transformed to glass.
Here does the pigeon or gull know of any honey
to which, for a share, it would lead a reverent man?
Here are the clouds produced from the livers of those who die,
or are they water vapor? It must be that they are vapor
for so many live here, so many die, the city would be continually buried
        in water,
as before the first day, if clouds rose from the dead.

My people too had a science and from the beginning.
From the opening of the story, when the bee carries D'xui over the
        flood
to lay him in the flower, we knew that there were no gods to intervene
        and answer,
only those contingent spirits, so small in the great after and before.
Though sometimes we shrank in their presence to tiny beetles,
they too grew often very small in ours.
Even the hunting stars, whose singing can be learned by men,
wander farther and farther, trailing their wounded prey,
to be lost in the black hills.
O husbands of the lynx, return.
But they don't listen, or can't hear.

2

So everything moves off and dies. Not only things
but what we said of the things.
The old story is no longer history.
But meanings are still quarried there, for nothing is true
and the human question is framed to have no answer.
And already this knowledge is known for one more myth,
we are already the ancients, deluded and long vanished,
only a mask in sand, paint on a rock,
and someone comes to disturb us, uncover us,

and say of us what we invented to say of all the dead:
that their knowledge was their consolation.

Or will those who come be different:
small gold-skinned people from the caves,
more skilled to read in dry remains
the history of strange races before the flood?
Such a people might say of us,
bending over our traces, not to defile them
with a touch or a breath: Those first ones lived when anathemas
infallibly won applause, and so were distracted.
They let themselves rail endlessly at injustice,
knowing that no one ever would be wrong,
there were so many standards of justification—
each always knew the charge was against his neighbor.
Meanings descended by millions into everything,
until they misunderstood all that they said.
Small groups would gather in locked rooms, talking,
and never come out again,
because the ones they followed had all died
and never returned. But this was better. For the teachings
the living drew from the dead were confused, unworthy,
taking no account of the rock rabbit's housewifery
or mantis, who perches on the eland's hoof to cross the desert.

Africa

Africa: perfect opposition,
perfect love. The angels of your god
are parrot, gourd and sounding log
and a severed head, preserved,
which shelters under its soft
dark hair as under wings
your volume, your augmented torrent
of unrooted sand, of wood asleep.

Your leaves made of flesh, your people
of reeds, reeds that can wander
in the forest, singing, remembering,
pausing to recite and build—
all luxuriate under light's sharp and idle hand
that lends confusion, vigor, marvels
to featureless blue. Blood gushes,

heated to blinding white before
your bellows. You are a martyr church,
your afterlife is the blazing
slow river in whose mud you perish,
the cracked plain, the absent herds,
all held in some mild gaze
that is happy, seeing what you are.

Still you dream of your failure,
of slavery drawn out
to the final generation, the first
abolishing note of brass
even harder, more flaming than your sky.
Perhaps even there you are condemned
by one you did not believe
for a work you did not perform.

From the fists which take from you,
which beat you and are sometimes yours,
you conceal yourself, like the new, fearful
potency of a boy in a crumbling house.
Out of your breast an image not yourself
rises, and far away
among leaves, insects and hidden birds,
alone, you fecundate what will be.

THE BEGINNING

Struck by the sun, I thought if everything burned and was forgotten
we would produce it all from the earth.
From freshness, from cleanness.
Across waving grasses that concealed no ruins
it would be a million years before Gilgamesh went seeking
beyond mountains and under rivers the survivor of the flood.
Would we attempt and always fail to surprise an unknown one
who walks in a garden, tending the pear trees?
There would be no stories yet, only amazement—
though we must notice soon that earth, the varieties of men and times,
are not inexhaustible, and days repeat:
even days before any creature has yet died.
But think of our feet on a soil in which no fathers lie.
Of the first to find his wife beside him, stiff, eyes open,
staring fixedly at the morning. And of that one who discovers
the skin may be torn from the living body, and beneath

is a fresh landscape of red and gray, streams and winding caves,
riven terrain of moving valleys and soft mountains.
Would he who committed the first simple murder be shown in waking
        dreams
the infinite length of the tradition he had founded?
To console his sleeplessness, would he travel and come
to plains of frost and establish peoples forever
dependent on artificial fire?
And perhaps no law created what has been,
but some chance error: standing on ground burnt clean,
we might not stumble again.
There would be other actions, and so other visions, explanations.
Yet say it were all repeated, the same pain, by will or need.
Still, to be the first—the first to wander,
so that no movement could ever be made by men
that had not already been ours: no ascent or decline,
no speech with another, no account of heaven or the atmosphere,
no taming of flocks, building of ships, invention of bread.
It is our word for desert, mountain, river,
they will seek forever in their many words.
Through the multiplication of their bodies and acts, they grope
as through shadows for our body struck by the sun.

THE WHEELWRIGHT

Unregarded now, the wheelwright perfects his art,

This wheel at which he has worked for sixty years—how it hobbles on
        its axle with the nervousness of gray streams, of squirrels on
        poisoned lawns, of a diplomat of snow posted to Africa.

It is not round—his whole art consists in his ancient hand covered with
        warts always spoiling the work of his smooth young hand.

He has used all the slopes of Oregon to make this tiny wheel that is lost
        in his palm,

This wheel the size of the gleam on an otter's back under a wooden
        bridge as a finch alights in a bush.

A woman watches from the bridge, a woman with the nails of a cat in
        place of eyelashes,

And she cries at the injustice that has been done her:

"My beauty is perfect except for this curse—invisible to the animals, but it turns men to steam,

And slices my cheeks if I close my eyes to sleep—I wake and my face is a world whose red lakes and rivers have congealed.

But at least I have dreamed that I am not a woman but a huge fish swimming under this bridge,

And someone leans over, spears me with his stick

And holds me up, transfixed and struggling, to fry near the sun.

And that sun is only a tiny shaded pool, shaped like the shell of love or the palm of a skeleton filled with water:

Green floating lilies, green air, and a single-jetted fountain, pencil-thin, breaking the stillness.

From far away comes a sound of cars and airplanes passing,

But I am gone,

A ghost within the light, within the colors and the mass of things, making them brood and remember like a man, though no man is here."

The night is wasting away,

And the wheelwright, too, feels himself vanish as he watches his fire

And the red strip of iron ready for shaping to a rim.

Slowly he dissolves into the metal's glow, into the impulse of the wild hammer as, unrestrained, it rises and falls, monotonously beating out the form.

Outside, the stars are devoured and moisture covers everything,

Dew deepening the rust on a blue sickle,

Which long ago someone forged under beech trees on the now ravaged
    slopes.

THE AIR HAMMER

Stained with red, the leaves were blown down
on the compressor that forged the air into blows
for the hammer breaking up the road. The pieces
were heaped into trucks and sometimes still a stretched
artery of tar linked one to another.

Children here, we slept in one room
where now the submachine gun rattle
attacks concrete. The nearness then
of your mystery, one day to be mine,
displayed but never divulged:
its skeletal image remains in me
of a soft human cleft in granite.

Will we at least be blown
against each other once again,
clenched in the same sweep
of a gray sky's trailing net?

In the vicinity of our childhood
houses diminish, vacant lots expand
and the days do nothing,
only hands work, conveying through idle time
bricks of the stairways, bridges, walls.

They are poured into hopper cars
and taken to the designated place
and there poured into pits.
Where water attacks the firmness of the land,
they support foundations
and good offices stand on the swamp.

The people who clean those buildings by night
swarm now from the district of our birth.
And here when they return
at dawn, the air hammer
crumbles and quarries their sleep.

Court

Slowly the hall fills up.
The shuffling newspaper boy
of fifty years,
his red ears beaten closed,
his speech
indecipherable static
of a ship lost at sea.
The midget bail bondsman
whose legs have no knees.
The detective whose heart once stopped
for a long moment,
who never speaks now or blinks
but totters daily through the old round,
a wooden doll on wheels
drawn by a thread.
And the female body that twitches,
still galvanized by hunger
or some memory, accused again today
of removing its shroud for hire.
The procession lengthens, flowing
to the court, and the watcher feels
that he is vanishing as it passes:
a thing like himself,
five-membered and symmetrical
around its sex, is only
an old idea of the earth's.

Before a Film

You stare at the blank screen:
a grayness without depth where soon
the images will pass out of nonexistence
and back again. And you will be lost
an hour in the spectacle of this life—
no matter how tedious, how badly made—
that fills, effortless and untired,
the space from its beginning to its end.

After its end, you will go out in the street
and be bored. Your attention will wander
among the pigeons, wires and signs,

dusk with its glowing orange shades:
mimicry of orange, color of all joyous or despairing
seasons of the day, and of mere calm—
the weight of fruit at noon.
Did this life ever begin, will it ever end?
And you go probing the crowds, the air,
the lamps, as if nearby is the screen
all's thrown against—and some blow might tear it,
and the beam of light with its struggling
gestures could pass through
and go out in the dark beyond.

FILM IN AN UNKNOWN TONGUE

Bangkok.
The naked god of love,
adolescent, violet-colored, scarred,
in his stiletto boat
conveys two Caucasian women.
Skiffs careen in the wash.
Paintless huts.
Children on mossy doorsteps.

At the stone lions the boatman,
smoking agèd engine in his hand,
delivers them.
The stairs come from under water
and beneath climbing sandals
the slime of another world,
lips exchanging moisture in darkness.

Who is that whitewashed statue
cracked and peeling,
in a toneless voice making impure proposals?
There is nothing in the human world
but women and that voice
seeking a living throat to speak it.

Nothing but women
and the sea swell at dusk:
the depths manifest in the surface,
bowels present in the skin
and its silk of light,

contentment in a motion as of hips,
a loose motion playing across
the day's rhythm,
a motion of breasts
molding eyes and hands.

Nothing but women and a vagrant light.

They are naked now
in the deserted garden
and their throats are pitchers.
Let us go down.
Nothing is moving now.
It is the freedom of which we dreamed.

O violation,
          beautiful youth,
once we were you.
Again now we feel that first anger
and the surprise of floating free.
Now in this palace of wood above the river
the plants tend themselves
and hope is the air.

Wine created the vessel
and the full vessel,
for someone to drink from it,
created man:
          even the man
who drinks from and refreshes
two Caucasian women
amid the gilding of cries and knives
and the cancer flowers.

The Ennui of Exegesis

Years after your actions have gone to bed,
patient study reveals to me
that coming as they did out of darkness
from a great distance like a falling shell
they fulfilled my intentions.

Curiously each day
a man watches a far-off hand
lift the fork or pistol to his mouth.
But news of you reached me only now and then,
a bird striking the window pane
so that I looked up from my book
and saw the messenger, stunned, stumble away,
having left the impression of violence,
brief collapse, and desertion.

Now the window is masked with fog. Out there
under the trees—the presumable
because remembered trees—what decisions
are being made? I handle a shell that lies
here on the desk: a mouth always speaking
the same word which who knows how to hear;
a head that is only a mouth with nothing
lying behind it, its thought
the light or darkness of the air.

Interpretations of silence, the various
silence, explode around. The room
is filled with craters cunningly arranged
as on dead moons, where men have wished to see
signs of intelligence. On the toothed horizon,
are those sporadic flashes signs from the others,
or effects of electricity in a cloud?

I wanted to make you love me,
but coincidence, in the main unfortunate,
replied to the messages I sent.
Each gesture attracted its riot
of joyous, angry and idiot response.
And are you seated, then, in the next room
in the quiet, waiting to be asked
the question as your dream intends it?

THE WAR

The war is comfortably furnished with my limbs.
The fear of what comes next created it
and here it is: the enmity
of right and left, crying like a beautiful beard

grown to cover a scar. The workmen send
a message up from below, that the engines
which in fact are only the ocean
vibrate on purpose to shake the rivets loose
and dump us playfully into the swimming pool.
We'll end up trying to breathe
in a sphere of water poured from our own mouths
(our mouths, the bursting fountains of the sea),
as heat shuts itself in the casket of ice it made.
Isn't this rather harsh, considering the offense,
that I haven't sent the thank you note,
that I can't dredge up amid these pink hats
and trumpet blasts any recollection
of the giver or the gift, though I feel certain
it is one of these things present in this room?
So much confusion. Even my wife
hates me because I want her
and don't recall who she is or is to be.
I look around at all these quiet women:
no lips move, no face rings a bell,
though to music her voice keeps saying my name,
the tones rising to indicate a question.

Prothalamium: Venus and Mars

It's the wedding day of our procedure
but his bride is the true conversation piece.
Faint blue and pink clouds glide down to nest
in the shell craters of her virgin cheeks and eyelids.
A beautiful woman to the waist, her nether parts
are a delicious, heart-rending serpent of ice cream
and the crowd cries as this confection
appears naked at the window. Between her breasts
is a strip mine known as Cupid's Landing Field.
The sad sympathy of her eyes waits
to be fired down the long barrels of her nose.
She turns: a flock of ashtrays rises clamorously
from the marsh of her wake
with a wild flurry of buttocks.
Look up! Divine love!
Every citizen from the mushroom to the meanest catfish
longs to be married today, and thus morals are strengthened
and thus the procedure is encouraged to proceed.

What a mob of uninvited guests has gathered in the plaza below!
It's touching to see the emotion of all that exiled royalty
for this commoner (this whore, some would say)
whom fate has lifted on their shoulders.
They wish the bridegroom's blessedness were their own.
Suddenly a rotten tomato smashes
against the bulletproof window of her balcony:
it's the tardy groom, arrived at last. But hurled forward
with all the crowd's desire, he has still missed the point.
Alas, though cultivated to be seedless
and plucked and dried for uncounted years,
he has proven too soft to penetrate her sanctuary.
Poor shattered prince!
And now who will marry her, who will be our king?
Nothing daunted, the frenzied people
stoop to nominate bricks and bottles.

Success attend you, O citizens.
May you find a new procedure,
though your next heroes in a similar fashion
become dust and pulp against that seductive smile.
Someday you will find the power worthy of this queen.
Someday you will reach her and your single state
vanish in the fiery cloud of the consummation.

The Villa of the Humanist Collector at Herculaneum

Born (so we may imagine him) with a foot turned inward,
he kept far-off from the heavy clash
of phalli and spears, the pounded track.
He came to know and amass these scrolls,
chiefly Epicurean and Stoic philosophers,
and to gather these torsos mythically twisted and lithe,
bodies still stretched after centuries
on the peak of desire among grape clusters
and the air breathed by painted flutes.

So now it comes to light, preserved:
knowledge that was counted lost, and some hint of him
who possessed it, chipped from the lava.
For stone, expelled from its homeland where
it runs like water, fell to this colder world
and was made ice.

Or he was a merchant, an administrator,
even a soldier who in youth
had slept naked in the snow
and received from boys and women
every impulse human nerves can transmit.
Still to him, if only in old age,
some compensation was necessary
in face of all that is placid and adequate
through beauty or strength, fecundity or sleep.

The gods are powerless, and living
as the skin fills with sand and twists the skeleton,
if only a man could know it, is a task.
Needless to revile yourself for days passing
as the youths with robes blown open
pass in the street; to doubt
if you possess the courage not to betray
beneath a Scythian blade. To each is posed
an equal challenge, even here
where nothing occurs but now and then
earth trembles a little—or is it your heart?

KEATS IN ROME

The tree of his lungs grows only fruit of blood
and the clear sky
deserts it, removing the air.
The birds carry off their music
and sexual solace follows them,
powerless in eternity,
in macelike beauty. All shapely things,
artifacts and ghosts of the gods
that sidle close to these old walls
in the hazy mornings, in the shadows,
reply with their ancient unforgiveness,
refuse to send him Lazarus
with a drop of water for a brittle tongue.

Delight in heaven's porch: nothing,
not hell, is as far from paradise.
Disease, they say, can unbuckle man from the wheel.
Awakening, he won't awaken again
to the birth of pleasure and fear: even this man,

who wrote the story of what always happens
everywhere in the earth. He hoped perhaps
to end it with the old sun's ascent,
Hyperion, triumph and restoration
of the exile. What stopped him:
inability to stop the sun in the sky?
Continual succession of days and other suns,
the story of what always happens
ends as it always ends,
coughing red clouds in the evening.

He wrote the story a second time to change it,
to show that all is within his body, is
his dream, and now, whether the sun
took the zenith for its eternal house
or fell crying again behind the mountains,
he would awaken at the end, though memory
preserve the threatened triumph of new gods.
But an old god triumphs, the story's end
written in the body.
And as ever, in the confused
romance of fever, the hero hates himself
for not having loved enough:
"I am guilty of my death, I burn
for not ending the story as I desired.
There is no death for one that loves the earth.
I wanted immortality to perfect
earth's gifts, and now the red mornings beg
some god to put a term to time's
endless decay. Is it only my weakness
that leaves this conclusion circling in the air?"

An hour and he will sleep or wake
free of the wheel, free of the little man
whom the leaf's gesture, the colored clay,
the beauty of women outlives.
Not their love but their loyalty is greater
to the failing earth.

The Golem

This prophet seems ill-content among his rats.
Yet he remains there scowling in the gutter,

naked on a bed of fruit rinds that seems to writhe,
and he gestures to anyone who passes near,
muttering something of politics and God's election.
No one can make out anything in his speech
beyond an islanded word or two in the babble:
"remnant," "abominations," "living creatures,"
"neat's dung for man's dung," "the son shall eat the father."
And if he means anything, it's probably
no more than all the prophets mean: that we,
like them, should give up comfort, duty, home,
and the hope of better days, of power over time,
which alone makes human life endurable.

Look close, some say, and you can see this man
is the same one, the charlatan, who vanished
many years ago—a magician the idle wives
would invite to teach the fashionable of power.
And it's true, this derelict might be the man.
I recall him in robes and jewelry, performing
for an assemblage of the rich and their hangers-on.
We were all, so then we said, seeking the door
to the limbo of serene mystery.

At first we would assemble in the halls
of merchants never at home—blazing caverns stuffed
with orthodox treasures: fables and acts of love
frozen in table legs and the gold frames of mirrors.
But soon, as we progressed (he said) in knowledge,
the man convened us elsewhere—
materializing unknown fruits in his palm
amid the ruins of a pottery kiln,
levitating by the piles of a rotten bridge.

One night as we were dressing for the dance
in feathers of African birds, he entered
and we went with him instead, though rain was falling,
on foot through lanes near the harbor
to a deserted district of small mills.
There in a dirt alley of gutted shanties,
he made a circle on the ground
and we were drawn around it like water to a low place,
unresisting. At once we felt the clay
assert itself in our flesh, and our faces
lose fineness, return to elementary daubs—

mouths mere gaps, eyes the shape of dry wells,
heads a crude outline that a child might draw.
Sky, earth and ocean seemed
to organize in spheres to the farthest distance
and strain against our ring. Within it,
with his spittle he mixed some mud,
breathing on his hands. The words he spoke to the lump
seemed random noises, yet we could feel them
part nerves and pluck at the spine.
The thing, too, as it augmented, beat
to their rhythm, which pulls and molds:
the head emerges, the lower body
is divided into legs, and breasts swell.
Then we see the left breast shiver—the voice
provides her with a heart. The walls of the shacks,
the sparse weeds and trees strain
to the point of bursting, spilling out their pulp
in the warp of the charm.

                        But now the philosopher
falls back exhausted. What can be done is done—
and she is less than four feet tall,
thicker than a dwarf, with toes and fingers
imperfectly separated, and a voice that croaked our words
or something like them—mysteries.
Each part of her resembled some part of us,
and we perceived new riddles, those of art,
the relation of image to thing and to idea.
Are things merely images? So I state it now,
but then it was a simple disgust.
We only watched her and thought of her in our beds.
Was this the pure product of desire,
the result of the will's dominion,
our dream, the vessel of perfect love,
perfect submission, made real—her eyes deep gouges,
her mouth a circle traced in mud,
her hand that an infant might have molded of clay
and left in the rain?

                        And yet she was immortal
and would serve him, the creator,
forever—when he cringed
and toppled away, she staggered after:
a thing born senile,

soon blending with the thick, silted lamplight.
And I thought the night sighed or laughed.

If this indeed is the same man, then where
is she? But still, the resemblance is so strong—
and maybe she's with him there, part of the offal
he crushes and hides beneath him in the ditch.
Having created such a loved one, such a love,
would it be a wonder if he now chooses this?—
living naked, cherishing rats,
drooling some fragments of God's word,
perhaps giving sign to the people, perhaps seeking
faith in the dirt of the roads.

IV   You, Whoever You Are

1

Fable of isolation and violence,
a man
where the crickets speak
to winter's open mouth:
the shadow of a nail
crawls among ripe blackberries,
their vines that bind and tear
swift feet. And soft
as breath at the closing
of a quiet sentence,
the September evening fills
with sickles, curved silhouettes
that fall toward the tangled
bank of the river. Your hand
falls over his, your palm,
cold from holding and offering
the violet air. And if a thought
desperate at the cranes returning
to their base in the shadows
blazes in him, this you harbor too
under cooling hills, as your molten
gold robed the breasts of trees
and a burning monster all day.

2

In you dark odors
and a sound of moisture and wind
flower, bringing to light
flesh that is the choired heads
of the grasses, the linked
fingers of numberless trees.

Is it solved in you, the desolating
scent of the uncovered ground?
The constant and sleep-denying rain
reveals an unquiet darkness,
water fleeing through the wrinkles
in yellow mud.

And the monotonous music of it prays
to you as to those powers
that have made life
interminable and too brief.

3

You too, fumbling here
with your hand that never closes.
Your isolation, hour of figures
cut from a spectrum in air,
crossing your palm, an expedition
of souls unborn. You watch,
your request limp on the slopes,
the bleaching sky, dark places
where a bride's moisture evaporates.
In a wooden house, all doors
and shutters open,
at times thrashing in a gust,
someone sits upright sleeping. Things
drift in his hand
under the avalanche of shadows.

4

Helpless in the amber and sleep
of your still life, you stir:
high leaves
in a wind that does not touch the ground,
or thistle exploding into flax.
But these things are your thought,
these and the mating butterflies
which pass so close to the sleeper's ear
that the sound of their wings brushing together
wakes him. How compare you
to your own thought? You sing
inwardly, struck by the sun,
meditate under gray sky, dream
in the moon's phases, let all things
sink back into strengthless memory
in the dark of the moon.
Never in its profusion
does your thought reach beyond itself.
Even the gesture of defiance, the leafless
tree gnarled like a fist thrust up
from a grave, rests perfectly within
its form of death. And our eyes
return effort to this stillness,
and to the living forms a desire
to burst the bounds of growth.
Our eyes: poor shoots
of the human seed, that old idea you had
to gather all in one reflection
with power to detach itself from the mirror
and live, and move, elsewhere.
Still you lie like a man and woman
in adjacent rooms. The heat
rises from the beds
and a hand seems hidden in the dark air
ready to appear and bless.
In the mind of each, all beauty
lies behind some door,
all emptiness is here. The trembling
of a paralysis, your drying
grass blades vibrate in place,
your birds move, either at random

or directed by pure need,
and some emblem of motion sleeps
in every fact of stillness.

5

After a fissure of sunlight
we spent ten years
walking among your dead
in the stone wind,
your amber breath
which their motions
turned gray. But even there
the blinded wall still ran
with vines and tongues.
In that weighted cloister
under the tattered ceiling
that sagged lower, no tendril
came to curl its light shade
on naked foreheads:
a night of oil
thickening in its swell.
But even so in a clearing
was a landing where we met
the lightest boat
and were carried onto the still river.
And below us a blue face
now and then would break
the mirror of black water.

6

In the scent of clover and hay,
in the pleasure of wild heat
subdued, a wet shade extracted out of fire
where the forest is crumbled
and drawn up again by light,

in all things most impervious
to the transmutation of thought
that falls in you, a hand
feeling darkly for an absent tool,

you meditate your aggression,
anarchy and silence. You hide your face
whose expression is peace
reflected from the sea that rolls and rots
a lost acorn cup, the ship of discoverers
offshore of a new world
where the trees appear far-off as flames of green water,
and where men's thoughts, ashore already,
are finding out tobacco and gold.

And sometimes you attack,
you rush out from every barrier
like a flood in a dream
where the furniture, the walls and floors
burst up, are water,
and startled the dreamer wakes
to the dry room, the bed
silent, not to affirm or to deny
that it is a ship of water
bearing a spirit of water
in the forms of the sea.

7

The lover is a dream you have.
Born of your brain, he strayed
through the things that happen there,
learning rhythms, expectancy,
and a pitiful few masks of the spring,
a few words of all
that winter, autumn and summer have to say.
In everything there were traces of your body,
as a voice heard
is the trace of an unseen speaker;
and he saw hands emerge,
one from the north, one from the south,
and exchange a sealed letter.
Why was there no one beside him?
So in your dream the lover
split himself in two
and the part that loved you
hated and wed the part
that took your place. You dreamed
that yet he would be born
and lie beside you. In your sleep,

in your dreams he cried out alone,
because you are the only other
and he is lost in you.

8

Why, if you have hidden from me,
do you linger where light
molds itself on green fingers,
on tattered hands
shading the tombs from the blaze
that denies all mercy, cutting out
the inscriptions and the drying grass?

Here you seem to walk.
I glimpse a flank, a stream
of hair turned green in the shadow,
passing between two stems—
you, or your image, pierced
by low fluttering notes.
And it seems possible: the legend
of water walking in human form
the waves of dust. You passed
almost unseen, but suddenly
the thought of death
was filled with a knowledge
of ghosts returning to bodies gnawed
for eons by greedy salt.
And my words, spoken
in anger and misery against men
who kill themselves with eyes open,
passed into your eyes
truly open, and returned to my mouth
as this air: milk of your breast.

9

Your voice:
first sign among dreamed remains
(shattered spectral walls obscuring
the city of perfected stone)
that images are of our eyes.

In it all history
was contradicted. Human, it called
for a being that moved, invisible
within the light, to intervene.
At dawn it muttered to slow worms
grazing on utter dark.

In sand moistened by the water's lip
was the root that, smothering,
clutches the murderer and cries...

your voice: desire.
And this alone distinguished you
from chill evenings at summer's ending,
from the earth.

10

Sometimes I imagine a crying face
dissolved above me...not in the rain
but in the hardest crystal,
the ruthless transparency that gives
the color of cold
to the purest light we know. No moisture
(dew or the rivers or storm)
is its crying, only the blankness among things:
the silence not of words unspoken
but of words unknown, the forms
curled on themselves in a necessary dream.

And its crying burns, self-fed,
in all the tongues for whom a single leap
is at once body and death.
A flash: one dies and another rises,
smaller, more distant, cool.
They are thrown back from their perimeters,
huddle together in the deepening walls
of charcoal. They have said almost nothing:
only a brittle complaint, a low insistence
snapping twigs, exploding the moist pebbles.
Yet already, under wet boughs, hissing
in green night, only a buried glow remains:
as if left for chance travelers to find
here, in the deaf music of the frogs.

11

Stay where you are, don't fly
still deeper in the self-absorption
of your wing, last livid shape
afloat on the wood's scaffold.
The fog that muffled
in cool mornings the river's warm
and almost silent throat
is removed now, burned
by the hand that sharpens apples
and mummifies the ones not eaten.
Now the glow that arouses pain
and brings it to such intensity that it dies
cracks the shield of its rusted lantern:
at last nothing is shaded
from the paleness it projects.
What is this white shell,
that the silent colors hurry to speak themselves
into its static curvings,
its diminished spectrum, shades of milk?
And will go on speaking despite
immobility, deafness, an absent bird
that broods over the ash.

12

Life you held on the palm
of your extended hand.
Why could our hands not close upon it?

Your gaze fell on us
from beyond a tangled curtain,
the yellow withes of the willow
trailing yellow leaves, from which we peered.
In the stream we glimpsed the reflection of an eye,
a glance setting fire to the ripples,
making things burst from themselves
as the flax bursts from the pods
which yet are motionless: it merely appears,
as the eye suddenly will pick out
a brilliant jay, frozen, watching in the vines.

And so to dusk, gradually assembling its dark empty bridge
into the heart of each thing.
And so to stillness, the end of us
travelers: children
who had now arrived and been annulled.
Yet out of that silence
and the place where there is no motion but communion
nevertheless anguish gathered itself, proceeded:

soon adult voices would shout our names, summoning.
Dinner would be ready,
although we had never been less hungry.

13

Always opening and closing,
your light sometimes a wall,
sometimes an eye, your air
either distance or a hand...
The birches filled with chaos
can mutter aloof, collecting
sparks without meaning,
pure instances of you.
Or in a corridor bees pass
and from high among drying needles
a brilliant dime
glazes the surface.
The greeting still returns
from vegetable words
to cellars where wings are a badge of foolishness
and the only tongue is human.
Among your stems, these leavings
half reclaimed by the rain and mud:
bottles, cigarettes, soaked papers,
photographs of women that someone pierced
with arrows and holes. On your path
so full of fluid openings
that inspire the light, this evidence
of a being to which everything is sealed.

14

When we wanted never to sleep again,
you brought us back
from the riot of unassembled blocks,
and every face that drew itself
on the black slate
of a doorless doorway.

Even the gnats
that burned their rootless schema above the path
rested in your eye.
A glance threaded the stems,
an arch opened
on the sky over a cemetery,
we were shown and we forgot
so many details of strange flesh
nervously bared and offered,
the way a cloud forgets its form.

Also we stumbled on heavy clouds
caught in shapes and fallen in wild wheat:
stones of an ancient wall
that once had lain on one another
without the aid of mortar.
In the afternoon
you withdrew them from your moist shadow.

15

Your high burials, your baths
made by a persistent torch
from the ruin of water,
your haze of curtains
burning and opening
on richer curtains—

a hand's attempts
to wipe the mist from the encrusted
window or mirror.

Why do you return so often
to this season that repays you
with dying, your own penny
tarnished with jealousy?
In the torrent you
are only a tiny raft,
a few saplings woven together,
still green, unaware you are dead, dragged
with chains to the empty sea.

Yet you admire the artistry
of the flood: a rock
worried to a statue of cancer,
a dwindling tower whose gaze
pursues a pheasant in the burning woods.
Even these, which a god would call
shapes of death, you hoard
in your sealed vault with each smallest
detail that crumbles from a life.

16

Abandoned, you return
to the place of the last meeting. Dying,
you summon a more than natural strength,
again compose yourself
to the beauty that was yours before the illness spoke,
before the betraying depths declared themselves
to the surface, to translucent skin,
the face that colors now
alternately with peace and desperation.

And all that is known of you,
the downward path, the unseen locust seized
in the midst of its chirring by a wasp,
the stars fleeing from every point,
the crimes committed at every point,

gathers in this last offering
you never refuse to make.
Still held and framed
in a vessel that vanished long ago,
let it gleam there, a shape of water,
a shape of clear sap and of blood

faintly reflecting our drying faces,
in every form of yours poised at our lips.

V   THE VISITATION

And Mary arose in those days, and went into the hill country with haste, into a city of Juda; and entered into the house of Zacharias, and saluted Elisabeth. And it came to pass that, when Elisabeth heard the salutation of Mary, the babe leaped in her womb; and Elisabeth was filled with the Holy Ghost: and she spoke out with a loud voice...

  First by a spasm that struck praise out of light
and now by weariness, thought and dreams,
I know you. This belly is shaken within,
a being without senses wields me
as a hand waves a piece of cloth
and gives me knowledge not mine of what you bear.
I feel how a small, boneless, floating thing
has dragged you here over the dog-yellow ridges
of hardened mud to this well and clutter of huts.
We are two wombs with tongues, thrown down
by some wave of lightless heat, pure desiccation,
the black noon of these hills made infinite.
We two, like those living bubbles, all stomach and mouth,
that the sea beaches in the blinding sunglare
to die, cast out, moving ever more feebly
to a remnant tide within them that dries away.
But the wave that leaves us in this desert
possesses us still and joys within.
There it makes itself new, another ocean
swarms with soft shapes suspended
over drowned mountains: an inner sea that moves
with its unseen life toward the female
gates of bone to be born, to cover the world.
And the promise there would be no second flood?
Already in the warp of our growing ocean's power
this burnt country, not made generous or less dry,
is changing to a spectral flood. You saw
in your coming how the weeds now are water-snakes,
the embedded stones become gray floating slugs
with eyes and slit mouths hidden in folded masses,
asleep on the swell that is God
or stricken Judaea—these waves of dust.

And so my age, with its brittle wrathful spine
twisting and crying as the womb's mass grows,
flails in my eyes, burning, softening, stretching
this too familiar place with such illusions.
Forgive me. This birth, this rod, has breached in me
a flood of dreams more bitter than itself.
Sometimes these images hide the common day
and make me long for barrenness again,
for the days of accusation to return
when I alone moved my limbs, devised and piled
my virtues though unblessed
by God and by a people fecund and bound.
But even then, turning in my daily track,
I would see a vision: headless men in the air
who beckoned and then would join my head
by a long cord to hovering wheels that spun
within each other without rhythm or speed
as I lifted water and ground corn.
All was a machine that touched nothing, a prisoner
confined by limitless space. Looking each day
at the stunted village, I knew my name, "the sterile,"
whispered by the forms that passed shrouded from heat.
There was harmony between the accusation
and the motionless mouths that made it—the sun
silent in the sky, and long silent too
the dull burning of the wives and priests.
What is a fruitless virtue? Does it exist?
My husband, before muteness froze him, priest,
chanted the daily psalms that were his censure:
blessèd the just, their wives are fruitful vines.
Either the promise is false or we were false.
But there were so many rituals and errors,
so many laws and such infinities
of evil reasons for obeying each,
and a depth of memory where every act and its reason
is lost and changes like a corpse in water...
therefore, nothing is ever proved against the promise
and we are always false. At last the people
ceased even to see me when I passed: they tired
under the rain of lashes for their own
intangible sins they gave me—leprosy, drought
and death falling on the faithful, until
in their boredom I disappeared, only another
proof that pain pursues unwilling crime.

I felt the light of seeing, a fresh pain,
in the eyes of girls alone. They still could dread me
fiercely, as a sign of what might come to them:
to fall endlessly away from the people
while seeming among them, side by side;
futile, to lose hold and tumble forever
in an empty well. Returning from the well,
the wives' talk still humming around my head,
I was swallowed often by the stare of the hills
bending down to smother the village, suck out
and bury in themselves all complaints,
all sons and daughters, births and illnesses
of the women: all were the buzzings of some flies
on a resinous weed somewhere in baking ravines.
All were barren, whether bringing forth bread from the oven
or a child from the womb. By morning it is eaten,
the task begins again, pounding, scraping, moistening.
The burning sun stands overhead, an impotent wife,
and watches us consume our children
as we stand behind the table and watch but cannot guard
the worn fathers, crumbling sons, at our bread.

   But at my pregnancy the people woke,
rejoicing as at rain. I too have joined
the knot of hands. But alone, I think: the strand
that spins itself from my body—what can he be?
Many years ago my parts of childbearing
were turned to dust,
dust thickened by blood to a muddy effigy,
like a child dissolved. It fell from me
drop by drop, limb by limb, dismembered, dead—
sole issue of my womb,
who never had been whole and living
but was only the ruin of agèd organs
where for a generation the human eggs
had risen through me and decayed.
Once long ago I thought they would give a daughter,
someone to live in the next house,
someone to draw and carry and pour with me
so much talking, a glossy stream
dissolving and carrying away the bitter salts
of the clay people, the earthen town:
we might have made it all sweet water

to irrigate the dusty slopes and bring here
grasses and trees and sheep
and the mild men who watch them.

  But now what thing divorced from all content
subsists in the dry, empty womb,
wrapped in no human fluid, no body's cloth,
not moored to maternal flesh or fed with blood?
He is falling toward us now, tumbling in his sea
of black space, swelling till he fills it all
and will burst through to earth.
The female ocean dried long ago in me:
he swims through some other water to Judaea—
waves of light that crest for frozen ages
and break, invisible, touching no shore. A light
disgorged by the burning being that swims in it
and is made from it, his will driven by it.
A light that is alone and so,
because it touches nothing, is pure darkness.
Then how can he find us here? But he approaches,
and in my old body already he loves the aging earth,
loves most the regions of silicon, flint and mica,
huge boulders orange in slanting light, the breeze
that crackles with a twilight waking of lions,
loud noises far away, the falling of heaped up rocks.
For a long time his flock will be the shadows
of desert bushes, tethered to their leafless poles,
always circling to avoid the sun.
A man dressed in skins, his bones porous with hunger,
eating insects from the ground, wild honey
that the birds find and bring him...

  These things I see...is a blindness wiped away?
Or is a veil dropped where hope and fear
project a future through the eye?
Now in the world I see approaching with him,
there are men and plants, animals and the fields,
but none have features. I distinguish
no faces or styles of dress,
tree is like tree and hour like hour.
This coming world: is it prophecy or remembrance?
As in a prophecy, all women
become one woman, all men one man,
there is only one thing of each kind and it is a word.

And whether they die, succeeding one another,
or endure forever in that landscape of blowing veils
where light drifts and merges...this image, our hope,
is it bleak or bright? A vast sphere
of whiteness that swallows all.

  But it is swallowed
by the first springing hair of a boy's beard,
the first droplet of blood from the severed foreskin.
It is the desert sea he carries in him
to bathe and irrigate again
in Jordan, that plain river of the earth,
to bring spectrum and feature out of blankness—
as if blood and a human glance returned
to a corpse advanced three nights toward pale clay.

  A headless corpse, its face the white of air.
The head is far away. Always I see it
as a lump of fire coal in a brazier, the black hair
curling downward, heavy smoke. The head
still lives, it feels across the wind, through walls,
to its body lying and calling a formless call
from the vacant neck, its feet wandering dustless slopes
while the mourners think they see them motionless
in death. And I am the one, with my fear, that does
this murder, in a dream I have awake
when the pain in my belly burns away
everything visible and leaves a slate to vision.

  Also I see how the baby will struggle from me,
the head emerge and dangle between my legs.
For a moment I am male, and it seems to me
there is, will be, no other male: only women like this
frozen in birth, the child not freed from the body,
hanging for a lifetime, never to grow,
always newborn and caught. Never will it be human,
but now and then a reminiscence of its proper form
will move it, and like a plant it rises
to the touch of sun or night,
the touch of warm air that moves across the fields,
the touch of women whose wombs are yet unblocked—
its hunger stirred by all things, all emptiness,
beyond it: even the hollow flesh where it is pinned.
At this my body shudders, the muscles clench

despite my will and love: the womb's mouth
closes on that soft neck in a spasm,
the head falls on the ground. For a long time
I gaze, not in horror or fear or any given peace.
My look encloses what is, what has become,
and it seems to me that this is my male child,
this already agèd head
that reddens the ground, its murdered lips
whispering some phrase from the prophets.
And my female child is his body now trapped in me
and rotting there to become at last
an excrement of blood-soaked dust.
My whole body is become a bowel:
below it voids these human fragments
with streams of urine, lumps of dirt;
above, such images and words.
Among all these holes that pour so generously,
where is one that will accept, a mouth to eat,
not speak? But I bring forth, unaided,
all these dreams from myself, as in the barren days;
my substance grows ever more exhausted,
my hollow more vast, an egg sucked out.

   It is the illusion of power, pure product
of maternal flesh that veers, when it meets a wall,
from luxury to death. Illusion: for by the child
I was chosen and I no longer live, it lives in me.
What power do I have on it except to kill?
But death is a power that only falls through me
from beyond, from the birthplace of the child.
With death, his twin, he eats my substance,
grows larger and nearer in the dark that heaves
and gleams already with an earthen aurora
reflected from barley, sharp green of sycamores,
the kindnesses of the earth he plunges toward,
olive trees cutting noon into feathered strips.
He rises from that ocean crying for water.
Why come to a desert to find water? Why burn
the dried out earth to ashes to create it?
Why go, taking my flesh, my blood and milk
wrung out of me, plundered while they are given?
A son should be bread from the flour made by our hands,
mixed to the ancient recipe, pressed into forms
as the wife prefers, and laid before...whom?

Her children?—other loaves. The child will eat the mother,
create himself, and with the flesh he digested
steal away to where a ceaseless rain of nails
claws it to tatters. I, mother, severed root
enduring in him an afterlife in salt-sown ground,
feel nothing in myself, receive through night and distance
the wounds in his limbs, or imaginations of wounds:
for who knows what he is in that future time,
if dead or living,
dying or in the act of getting a child?

   Perhaps he still works beside the muddy river
and pilgrims returning sometimes tell me of him.
Perhaps the soldiers have not yet arrived.
Still the camel drivers at the ford, the weary
foreign traders, farmers and shepherds of that region
gather around him with boredom, laughter, attention,
a day-long wondering sorrow, a crowd's fly-murmur
of miracles and the market for woolen cloth,
while he is speaking. This absent son,
how does his absence differ for us from death?
Who knows that someone distant beyond the eye
is living? Only, not knowing him dead,
our hope expects him here tomorrow
and shows him to us, far-off but on the earth,
fulfilling ancient customs and speaking
with women and men in the syllables long assigned.
He must still live between familiar clay and sky,
and the eager heart knows: nothing will change,
forever he will talk with drovers and merchants
on Jordan's bank in robes more dust than cloth,
joking at his sores, expecting death,
searching for the new in each cracked, ancient face,
always to be found if there is need to feel his hand.

   This is what is. The new that he announces,
how will he find it? All is foreseen.
The work goes forward alone: our hands must follow.
The weight of the child in me made the sight of people
heavy, I was driven to change my hour
at the well from crowded noon to night,
cooler and emptier but without rest
and crossed by other signs, darker, more silent.
I would hoist my jar, blue-black, a part of night,

and carry it through slaughtered flocks that seemed
to lie in the streets: dull gleaming of white stones,
or moonlight on dust, or images of the wives
asleep in their houses. Then, plunging
the bucket into the dewless, deserted quiet,
I would hear it fall and clatter on rock: the well
full since Joshua, full this afternoon,
is dry now and has been dry a thousand years.
Across the shrouded ridges, the tiers of flint,
in the river scar, the winds end, the water falls.
I am so old, so dry with child, my bones
will snap if I lift the bucket, even filled
with dryness, nothing, shadow—yet I pull,
feeling the rope will draw me down. The bucket
rises and totters on the stone. And in it:
nothing but a word, and a tiny shape to speak it,
and a scream, almost inaudible. The dry container
holds a crude wooden knife with crossing haft...
or it might be man with arms extended,
or a sword that has pierced its man
from head to feet and grown with him
into one being: incision, body and pain.
Between the knife and the cry I hear the word:
"He who has seen his brother has seen God."

  So then I know my son and yours are dead
already, before their births, and you and I
are dead. Because I am your brother,
and Zacharias, this mute stock, is our brother,
and the women day upon day at the well are God.
What can we do for them or for ourselves?
What power is in us? To be the hardened channel
of further children, more brutal dreams?
This is the end of the birth pain: to bring forth
such gods as ourselves. At the revelation
I grow still older and drag the growth
within me back through the violet streets.
I set down the empty jar so like the night...
and in the morning it is filled with water:
plain water, that does not replenish itself or cure
disease, or even quench our thirst. Another
sign without issue, another impotent marvel
that might be my dream or fever or any veil.

At the child's conception I felt the power
go out of me. All ended
in enormous heat that consumed the desert,
a flood more salt than water, vaster than the night sky.
Now in a heated torrent, a whirlwind of dust,
he is passing on his way to be born and die,
and the trees in his wake will be reduced to scaffolds,
shafts with crossbars stabbed into the slopes.
Illusion is burnt away
and men are scaffolds, and cities, temples, mountains.
The soul of each thing is bared: a skeleton,
two lines that cross, banal geometry
from which the flesh falls, leaving obedient bone.
Why in the promised splendor of these births
does this old shadow threaten me with the law?
The tree-man in the well, one with his gibbet,
man in the form of a sword—I see him now
piercing or growing from your eyes, limbs, heart.
Your simple look flows with blood.
A senile dream, the lust and malevolence of my spine,
learns it is dying under that strict sky
and rests its stiffened tongue in me. And earth:
its future is only pride that molds itself
to a disease's dream of vigor. It seduces the dying
and its crumbling brings out of me a true prophet,
the impassive brilliance of words followed by blood,
under the age-old scattering
of haughty ash. And empty space, which grows
ever more like itself if we feed it,
treasures only your eyes for witnesses
of tedium kindling there a willing star.

Author's Note

Early Poems reprints poems written 1966–77; they appeared in periodicals and chapbooks 1973–80 and in books 1975–83. I have corrected typographical errors and made a few authorial changes, small ones except in the cases of *New Poems* (1974) and *Here* (1975): some of the poems from these books are presented in revisions made 1977–78. The contents of *Here* are rearranged, and several poems retitled, in accordance with a version prepared in 1978 for a second edition (1980) on cassette tape; at that time, a nine-part sequential poem was replaced with an earlier four-part version. Poems from *New Poems* and *Here* that were republished in subsequent books have been left in their later positions. *New Poems* originally contained "Permanence of Evening" (*Between the Root and the Flower*), "Romance" (*Black Orchid*) and "As I Understood It" (*Here*). *Here* originally contained four poems now in *Black Orchid*: "The Problem," "Fields in the Air," "Memories of a Small Town Childhood" and "Modern Love."

The books included in *Early Poems* are:
New Poems (Boston: Swan Song Books, 1974)
Here (Portland, ME: Contraband Press, 1975, 1980)
Black Orchid (Toronto: Dreadnaught Inc., 1981)
Between the Root and the Flower (White Rock, BC: Blackfish Press, 1982)
The Visitation (Toronto: Aya Press, 1983)

Chapbooks incorporated in whole or part in these books are:
Catalogue of Bourgeois Objects (New York: Some, 1977)
Water Follies (London, ON: Killaly Press, 1978)
Signs and Certainties (Montreal: Villeneuve Press, 1979)
The Death of Francisco Franco (White Rock, BC: Blackfish Press, 1979)
Keats in Rome (Montreal: Ll Editions, 1980)
Music and Exile (Toronto: Dreadnaught Inc., 1980)

Between the Root and the Flower is in memoriam Rosanne Moritz, 1953–1979.